American Short Stories
1920 to the Present

PROGRAM PLANNING GUIDE

Perfection Learning®

EDITORIAL DIRECTOR	Julie A. Schumacher
EDITOR	Terry Ofner
ART DIRECTOR	Randy Messer
DESIGN	Robin Elwick, Emily J. Greazel

Copyright ©2007 by Perfection Learning Corporation
P.O. Box 500
Logan, Iowa 51546-0500
Tel: 1-800-831-4190 • Fax: 1-800-543-2745

Printed in the United States of America

1 2 3 4 5 6 PP 12 11 10 09 08 07

75709
ISBN-13: 978-0-7891-7076-7
ISBN-10: 0-7891-7076-0

Contents

To the Teacher: One Size Doesn't Fit All 1

Customizing the Matrix Program 2

    1. Choose a Literature Anthology 2

    2. Add Supplemental Literature 3

    3. Choose a Language Handbook 4

Differentiated Instruction 5

Flexible Grouping 7

Lesson Planning with the Matrix Program 9

    Suggested Full-Year Plan for the *American Short Stories* Matrix Program (chart version) 10

    Suggested Full-Year Plan for the *American Short Stories* Matrix Program (text version) 12

    Full-Year Template 14

    Sample Unit Plan 16

    Unit Plan Template 18

    Weekly Lesson Plan Template 19

    Daily Lesson Plan Template (Form A) 20

    Daily Lesson Plan Template (Form B) 21

    Daily Lesson Plan Template (Form C) 22

    Differentiated Instruction Lesson Template 23

Matrix Components 24

American Short Stories, Table of Contents 25

American Short Stories, Essential Selections 27

American Short Stories Teaching and Assessment Resources, Sample Pages 29

American Short Stories, Related Longer Works 43

Literature & Thought, The Harlem Renaissance, Table of Contents 47

Literature & Thought, The Harlem Renaissance, Teacher Guide, Sample Pages 49

Literature & Thought, Times of Change: Vietnam and the 60s, Table of Contents 50

Literature & Thought, Times of Change: Vietnam and the 60s, Teacher Guide, Sample Pages 52

The Essential Guide to Language, Writing, & Literature, Blue Level, Table of Contents 53

The Essential Guide to Language, Writing, & Literature, Blue Level, *Teacher Guide*, Sample Pages 57

Matrix Program Titles 60

Many Voices Literature Anthology Titles 61

Literature & Thought Titles (with Essential Questions and Featured Thinking Skills) 62

Parallel Text Titles 65

Retold Titles 65

TO THE TEACHER:
One Size Doesn't Fit All

The Perfection Learning Matrix program has been designed to provide the middle school and high school educator with a comprehensive, easy-to-manage language arts program.

For the study of literature, the wide selection of anthologies, supplemental literature collections, novels, and dramas allows each classroom curriculum to be specifically based on student needs and abilities, rather than the dictates of a "one size fits all" approach.

The addition of skill-based materials in grammar, composition, vocabulary, and reading completes the curriculum.

And finally, the Matrix program provides teacher materials that are intelligent, useful, and straightforward rather than overblown and redundant.

This Program Planning Guide is intended
- to describe the various components of the program.
- to illustrate how pieces of the Matrix work together to create a comprehensive language arts curriculum.
- to suggest ways in which curriculum can be developed using the Matrix components.

CUSTOMIZING THE
Matrix Program
Is as Easy as 1, 2, 3

Follow this simple 3-part process to customize your program.

I. CHOOSE A LITERATURE ANTHOLOGY

See complete **Table of Contents** and **Essential Selections** on pages 25–28.

- *Many Voices* literature anthology, *American Short Stories: 1920 to the Present* (552 pages)

  —four units of American short stories organized by decades

  —reflects literary, social, and historical periods

  —a focus on the style of important American writers

  —strong emphasis on writing integrated throughout the text

See **samples** on pages 29–42.

- *American Short Stories Teaching and Assessment Resources.*
  The literature anthology *American Short Stories* is accompanied by a manual that contains extensive teaching suggestions, reproducibles, and assessments for each selection. Following is a partial list of these resources.

Teaching Pages
—Skill Charts
—Anticipation Guide
—Differentiated Instruction Activities
—Selection Teaching Pages
—Unit Writing Prompts and Project Suggestions
—Evaluation Rubrics
—Related Literature Suggestions

Student Reproducibles
—Active Reading Model
—Active Reading Practice
—Unit Introduction Activities
—Unit Vocabulary Lists
—Comprehension Quizzes
—Literary and Reading Skill Development
—Vocabulary Quizzes
—Unit Tests
—Writing Workshops

2. ADD SUPPLEMENTAL LITERATURE

• *Literature & Thought.* 22 titles, 144 pages each
  —each title focused on an essential question
  —mixed genre literature groupings
  —direct teaching of critical thinking
  —Teacher Guides available for all titles

*See **complete list of titles** on pages 62–64.*

*See page 65 for **a complete list of titles.***

• *Parallel Texts.*
  Original text and modern
  translation on facing pages
  —9 Shakespeare titles
  —early American literature
  —early British literature
  —Teacher Guides available for all titles

• *Retold* Titles. Respectful adaptations of
  classic stories, novels, myths, and folktales
  —addresses the needs of
    struggling readers
  —teacher resources help develop
    skills in reading, vocabulary,
    writing, and literacy

***For titles,** see page 65.*

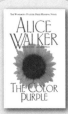

*See **related works** to accompany **American Short Stories** on page 43.*

• Classroom books
  —choose from thousands of
    fiction and nonfiction titles
  —teacher resources and assessments
    available for many of the most
    popular works

See complete **Table of Contents** on pages 53–56.

See **sample pages** on 57–59.

3. CHOOSE A LANGUAGE HANDBOOK

- *The Essential Guide to Language, Writing, & Literature*
    —Red Level, targeted for middle grades
    —Blue Level, developed for secondary students

- *The Essential Guide to Language, Writing, & Literature*, Teacher Guide. The handbook Teacher Guide contains a variety of instructional ideas, suggestions, and resources for presenting the lessons. The main features include:
    —References to Additional Resources
    —Objectives
    —Create Interest (warm-up activities)
    —Guided Instruction
    —Connect to Everyday Life activities
    —Differentiated Classroom activities
    —Collaborative Learning
    —Stumbling Blocks
    —Integrating Technology
    —Workplace Writing

- Grade-level language skillbooks for the following language arts strands are available:
    —Grammar, Usage, & Mechanics
    —Vocabulary
    —Test Preparation

- *Assessment Resources*, Red and Blue Levels, contain:
    —Pretests and Chapter Tests for all handbook chapters
    —End-of-course tests
    —Rubrics
    —Student Models

- 6 Trait Power Write
    —Online writing program using the 6 Traits assessment model
    —Strategies for 23 forms of writing
    —Comprehensive classroom management component

- *Image Grammar Activity Book*
    —Innovative approach authentically integrates grammar and writing
    —Extensive teacher materials in both print and CD-ROM versions
    —Classroom PowerPoint presentation on CD-ROM

DIFFERENTIATED
Instruction

DEFINITION

"The intent of differentiating instruction is to maximize each student's growth and individual success by meeting each student where he or she is, and assisting in the learning process."

www.enhancelearning.ca

*See examples of **differentiation activities** on pages 32–33.*

STUDENT LEARNING PROFILES

In order to provide a successful learning experience for each student, teachers need to consider the following questions as they develop curriculum:

- What is each student's language proficiency?
- What prior knowledge and experiences does each student have?
- What is the student's preferred learning style?
- What are the student's interests?
- What is the emotional and social development of the student?

Differentiated Instruction

Unit One: Literature from the 1920s to the 1940s

Discuss with students the overview of American history from 1920 to 1950 on pages 18–19 of the student book. Also, ask them to contribute any information they might have about the subject matter of the photographs on these pages as well as those on pages 16–17. To set the mood for the selections, play recordings of popular music from this time period, such as the music of Louis Armstrong, Glenn Miller, and Duke Ellington.

Differentiated Classroom Tip:

With a longer, more difficult selection, arrange students into groups of five or so, mixing their learning styles and abilities. Assign each one a different aspect of the selection to investigate, for example, theme, plot, character motivation, setting, or viewpoint. Each member of the group researches the assignment at his or her own reading level. Then groups split up so that all students investigating the same aspect compare notes and teach one another. Finally, students return to their original groups so that every member of each group can report to the others and share their knowledge.

*Sample page from **American Short Stories Teaching and Assessment Resources***

Name of Selection	TYPE OF LEARNER			
	Auditory	**Visual**	**Kinesthetic**	**ELL/Struggling**
In Another Country pp. 21-27 Easy	Have students read the story aloud to one another. Encourage discussion as they read.	Ask students to draw or paint a view of 1940s Milan, based on the descriptions in the first few paragraphs of the story.	Have students try to recreate the exercises the soldiers were asked to perform with the machines at the hospital.	Help students interpret the meaning of the story by focusing on the significance of the major's words, "I am utterly unable to resign myself."
He pp. 20-	Assign two students the	Have students draw a	Have students pantomime	Discuss with students

AREAS OF DIFFERENTIATION

When developing strategies for differentiating instruction, there are four possible approaches:

DIFFERENTIATION STRATEGIES

• *Anticipation Guides*
• *Study/Reading Buddies*
• *Graphic Organizers*
• *Peer Tutoring*
• *Anchoring Activities*
• *Independent/*
  Group Studies
• *Tiered Assignments*
• *Concept Mapping*
• *Journaling*
• *Portfolios*
• *Authentic Assessment*
• *Adaptation to*
  Learning Style

Details and definitions for these and other strategies can be found on many of the Web sites below.

• **Vary the content.** Students of differing abilities may master the same learning goals and objectives even though they use separate instructional materials, take varying amounts of time to complete their work, and reach greater levels of complexity in the subject matter.

• **Vary the process.** Teachers should use a wide range of teaching strategies so that all students can master instructional objectives. These techniques include direct instruction, inquiry-based learning, cooperative learning, and other strategies such as graphic organizers, mapping, and scaffolding. (*See* "Differentiation Strategies" suggestions at left.)

• **Vary the product.** The product that students produce to demonstrate mastery of a concept should vary depending on such determiners as the student's abilities and preferred learning style. Realistic expectations for students who work below grade level will allow them to experience success, while advanced students should be challenged to produce more complex work.

• **Vary the activities.** While no teacher can create individual activities for every student and every objective, it is important to provide options when possible. The chart on the previous page shows a variety of activities for a selection in the *American Short Stories* anthology. All teacher materials for *Many Voices* anthologies provide differentiation activities. (To examine activities from the *American Short Stories Teaching and Assessment Resources*, see pages 31–42 of this guide. The same types of activities are included in teacher materials for *The Essential Guide* language handbook. Sample pages can be found on 57–59.)

WEB SITES FOR INFORMATION ON DIFFERENTIATED INSTRUCTION

• www.teach-nology.com/tutorials/teaching/differentiate
• www.cast.org/publications/ncac/ncac_diffinstruc.html
• www.ascd.org/portal/site/ascd/
  menuitem.3adeebc6736780dddeb3ffdb62108a0c
• www.help4teachers.com/samples.htm
• www.enhancelearning.ca/differentiating.html
• www.internet4classrooms.com/di.htm
• www.teach-nology.com/litined/dif_instruction/
• www.weac.org/kids/1998-99/march99/differ.htm
• www.sde.com/Conferences/Differentiated-Instruction/DIResources.htm
• http://tst1160-35.k12.fsu.edu/mainpage.html
• http://ericec.org/digests/e536.html

FLEXIBLE
Grouping

One of the best ways differentiation can be effective is through grouping students according to their ability, their favored learning style, or the product/activity at hand.

As you integrate supplemental literature into the study of the core anthology, there may not be time for all students to read all selections. Several strategies can be used to limit the number of selections read by each student yet still ensure that each reader experiences the richness of the cultures in each geographical region.

COOPERATIVE GROUPING

Step 1 – Study Groups

Arrange students in heterogeneous cooperative study groups of 3–5 people. Each group will read 4 or 5 selections from the unit, predetermined by you.

After reading each selection, the group should discuss the selection questions. You might also want them to consider broader questions such as the following:

1. What styles or themes do the stories have in common?
2. How are the stories different?
3. What do you admire about the stories you read?
4. What, if anything, surprised you?

This group should meet for 2 to 3 days. The actual reading could be done in class or as homework.

Step 2 – Discussion Groups

Rearrange the students into groups with at least one representative from each cooperative study group. Have students share what they learned and take notes as they listen to others.

Teacher Role: Monitor the groups to check progress and offer assistance if the members are having comprehension questions with either the selection or the questions.

LEVELED GROUPING

Step 1

Arrange students homogeneously in groups of 3 or 4 according to reading ability levels. Using the chart of difficulty levels on pages 32–33 of this guide, assign 3 to 4 selections that match the level of the group members.
All groups should answer the same set of questions after reading each selection, as described in Cooperative Grouping above.

Step 2

Same as Step 2 for cooperative groups.

Teacher Role: Monitor the groups to check their progress and offer assistance when necessary. Groups with the easiest selections should be monitored more closely than the other groups.

ESSENTIAL SELECTIONS

Both the *Many Voices* anthologies and the *Literature & Thought* anthologies identify significant selections from each unit or cluster that will give readers the essence of the unit without reading every selection. Pages 27–28 of this guide include the essential selections for *American Short Stores: 1920 to the Present*. Each *Literature & Thought Teacher Guide* lists the essential selections on page 7. This page also provides a lesson plan for a 1- to 2-week study of the anthology. A sample of this material can be found on page 49 of this guide.

LESSON PLANNING WITH THE

Matrix Program

On the following pages you will find suggested plans for a full year of integrated studies using Matrix materials, as well as sample plans for individual units. In addition, various blank templates are provided to assist you in developing plans that meet your specific curriculum requirements.

Suggested Full-Year Plan for the *American Short Stories*
      Matrix Program (chart version) 10

Suggested Full-Year Plan for the *American Short Stories*
      Matrix Program (text version) 12

Full-Year Template 14

Sample Unit Plan for the *American Short Stories* Matrix Program . . 16

Unit Plan Template for the *American Short Stories* Matrix Program . . 18

Weekly Lesson Plan Template 19

Daily Lesson Plan Template (Form A) 20

Daily Lesson Plan Template (Form B) 21

Daily Lesson Plan Template (Form C) 22

Differentiated Instruction Lesson Template 23

SUGGESTED FULL-YEAR PLAN FOR THE *AMERICAN SHORT STORIES* MATRIX PROGRAM

This suggested plan is anchored by the literature anthology *American Short Stories* and the language handbook *The Essential Guide to Language, Writing, & Literature,* Blue Level. This plan can be easily adapted to the needs of your students and your curriculum requirements. A blank grid for creating your own plan can be found on pages 14 and 15 of this Planning Guide.

Week	Anthology: *American Short Stories*	Handbook: *The Essential Guide,* Blue Level		Supplemental Literature	Novels & Other Longer Works
		Writing	**Language Arts**		
1	**Unit 1** Literature from the 1920s to the 1940s	Review as needed: **Chapter 20** Persuasive Writing **A Guide to Literary Analysis**	Review as needed: **Chapter 9** Capitalization **Chapter 10** End Marks and Commas **Chapter 11** Italics and Quotation Marks **Chapter 12** Other Punctuation		
2					
3					
4					
5				**Literature & Thought** *The Harlem Renaissance*	
6					
7		**Synthesis Essay**	**Chapter 29** Critical Thinking		
8					
9					***The Great Gatsby*** F. Scott Fitzgerald
10					
11					
12	**Unit 2** Literature from the 1950s and 1960s	**Chapter 21** Writing About Literature	**Chapter 5** Using Verbs **Chapter 6** Using Pronouns		
13					
14				**Lit. & Thought** *Times of Change: Vietnam and the 60s*	
15					

Week	Anthology: *American Short Stories*	Handbook: *The Essential Guide,* Blue Level		Supplemental Literature	Novels & Other Longer Works
		Writing	Language Arts		
16				**Lit. & Thought** *Times of Change: Vietnam and the 60s*	
17					
18					***Death of a Salesman*** Arthur Miller
19					
20	**Unit 3** Literature from the 1970s and 1980s				
21					
22					
23		**Chapter 22** Creative Writing	**Chapter 8** Using Adjectives and Adverbs		
24					
25					***The Color Purple*** Alice Walker
26					
27					
28	**Unit 4** Literature from the 1990s				
29					
30		**Chapter 23** Writing the Research Paper			
31					
32					
33					
34					

SUGGESTED FULL-YEAR PLAN FOR THE *AMERICAN SHORT STORIES* MATRIX PROGRAM

(This is a text version of the full-year chart that appears on the previous two pages.)

WEEKS 1–4

Literature: *American Short Stories*
   Unit One: Literature from the 1920s to the 1940s
The Essential Guide Writing
   Review Chapter 20: Persuasive Writing
   Review "A Guide to Literary Analysis"
   Writing Assignment: Persuasive Essay
The Essential Guide Language Arts
   Begin review of Chapters 9–12: Capitalization and Punctuation

WEEKS 5–8

Literature: Supplementary Text
   The Harlem Renaissance, Literature & Thought Series
   Writing Assignment: Synthesis Essay
The Essential Guide Language Arts
   Complete review of Chapters 9–12
   Chapter 29: Critical Thinking

WEEKS 9–11

Literature: Suggested Longer Work
   The Great Gatsby by F. Scott Fitzgerald

WEEKS 12–17

Literature: *American Short Stories*
   Unit Two: Literature from the 1950s and 1960s
Literature: Supplementary Text
   Times of Change: Vietnam and the 60s, Literature & Thought Series
The Essential Guide Writing
   Review Chapter 21: Writing About Literature
   Writing Assignment: Short Literary Essay
The Essential Guide Language Arts
   Chapters 5–6: Using Verbs & Using Pronouns

WEEKS 18–19

Literature: Suggested Longer Work
   Death of a Salesman by Arthur Miller

WEEKS 20–24

Literature: *American Short Stories*
  Unit Three: Literature from the 1970s and 1980s
The Essential Guide Writing
  Review Chapter 22: Creative Writing
  Writing Assignment: Short Story
The Essential Guide Language Arts
  Chapter 8: Using Adjectives and Adverbs

WEEKS 25–27

Literature: Suggested Longer Work
  The Color Purple by Alice Walker

WEEKS 28–33

Literature: *American Short Stories*
  Unit Four: Literature from the 1990s
The Essential Guide Writing
  Review Chapter 23: Writing the Research Paper
  Writing Assignment: Research Paper

FULL-YEAR TEMPLATE

Week	Anthology: *American Short Stories*	Handbook: *The Essential Guide*, Blue Level		Supplemental Literature	Novels & Other Longer Works
		Writing	Language Arts		
1					
2					
3					
4					
5					
6					
7					
8					
9					
10					
11					
12					
13					
14					
15					
16					
17					

Week	Anthology: *American Short Stories*	Handbook: *The Essential Guide,* Blue Level		Supplemental Literature	Novels & Other Longer Works
		Writing	Language Arts		
18					
19					
20					
21					
22					
23					
24					
25					
26					
27					
28					
29					
30					
31					
32					
33					
34					
35					

SAMPLE UNIT PLAN FOR THE AMERICAN SHORT STORIES MATRIX PROGRAM

Unit	Unit Theme	Literature Text and Teacher Materials	Supplemental Reading	Literature and Reading Skills	Writing	Language Arts Text
Unit One: Literature from the 1920s to the 1940s 4 weeks	Appreciate Writer's Craft and Style	*American Short Stories* Unit One **Differentiation** _Average and Above Average_ All unit selections _Below Average_ Choose from Essential Selections list on pp. 27–28. *See also.* **Differentiated Instruction Activities,** pp. 44–46 of *American Short Stories Teaching and Assessment Resources* book.		From *Teaching and Assessment Resources* book. Reading Skills <u>Active Reading Strategies;</u> Active Reading Model; Vocabulary Handout. Literature Skills irony, mood, point of view, local color, fable, appearance vs. reality, mysterious stranger theme, the unreliable narrator, symbolism, the antihero, pathos, the cautionary tale, enigma	**Persuasive Essay** Instructor assignment or student choice from prompts on p. 163 of *American Short Stories* and/or Writing Prompts on pp. 79–80 of *Teaching and Assessment Resources* book. **Differentiation** <u>Above Average</u> Longer paper (approx. 1500 wds.) <u>Average</u> Shorter paper (approx. 5 paragraphs) <u>Below Average</u> Paragraph	*The Essential Guide to Language, Writing, & Literature,* Blue Level Review Capitalization and Punctuation (Chapters 9–12). *Grammar, Usage, & Mechanics Skillbook* Select appropriate practice as needed. Chapter 20: Persuasive Writing "A Guide to Literary Analysis" **Differentiation** _Below Average_ Review Chapter 13: Introduction to the Process of Writing and Chapter 14: The Six Traits of Good Writing.

SAMPLE UNIT PLAN FOR THE AMERICAN SHORT STORIES MATRIX PROGRAM

Unit	Unit Theme	Literature Text and Teacher Materials	Supplemental Reading	Literature and Reading Skills	Writing	Language Arts Text
Unit Two: The Harlem Renaissance 4 weeks	Connect literature to history through the essential question: *What was the Harlem Renaissance?*		*Literature & Thought, The Harlem Renaissance* **Differentiation** *Average and Above Average* All *Literature & Thought* selections *Below Average* Choose from Essential Selections list on p. 7 of *The Harlem Renaissance Teacher Guide.*	From *American Short Stories Teaching and Assessment Resources* book. Reading Skills <u>Active Reading Strategies;</u> <u>Active Reading Model;</u> Vocabulary Handout. Literature Skills irony, mood, point of view, local color, fable, appearance vs. reality, mysterious stranger theme, the unreliable narrator, symbolism, the antihero, pathos, the cautionary tale, enigma	**Synthesis Essay** Instructor assignment or student choice from prompts on p. 142 of *The Harlem Renaissance* and/or Writing Prompts on pp. 55–57 of *The Harlem Renaissance Teacher Guide.* **Differentiation** *Above Average* Longer paper (approx. 1500 wds.) <u>Average</u> Shorter paper (approx. 5 paragraphs) <u>Below Average</u> Generalization essay of 1 to 3 paragraphs based on prompts from p. 76 of *The Harlem Renaissance.*	*The Essential Guide to Language, Writing, & Literature,* Blue Level Complete review of Capitalization and Punctuation (Chapters 9–12). *Grammar, Usage, & Mechanics Skillbook* Select appropriate practice as needed. Chapter 29: Critical Thinking

UNIT PLAN TEMPLATE FOR THE *AMERICAN SHORT STORIES* MATRIX PROGRAM

Unit	Unit Theme	Literature Text and Teacher Materials	Supplemental Reading	Literature and Reading Skills	Writing	Language Arts Text

WEEKLY LESSON PLAN TEMPLATE

INSTRUCTOR _____ CLASS _____ WEEK OF _____

	Literature	Language Arts	Other
MONDAY			
TUESDAY			
WEDNESDAY			
THURSDAY			
FRIDAY			

DAILY LESSON PLAN TEMPLATE (FORM A)

INSTRUCTOR _____ CLASS _____ WEEK OF _____

Standards/Objectives

Materials Needed

Procedures/Activities

Differentiation

Assessment

DAILY LESSON PLAN TEMPLATE (FORM B)

INSTRUCTOR _____ CLASS _____ WEEK OF _____

Standards/Objectives	

Lesson	Assessment	Assignment/Homework

DAILY LESSON PLAN TEMPLATE (FORM C)

INSTRUCTOR _____ CLASS _____ WEEK OF _____

	Literature	Language Arts
STANDARD/ OBJECTIVE		
TEXT		
CLASSWORK		
HOMEWORK		

DIFFERENTIATED INSTRUCTION LESSON TEMPLATE

INSTRUCTOR _____ CLASS _____ WEEK OF _____

Subject	Rationale	Strategy

Differentiate What?	Differentiate How?

Resources Needed	Approximate Time to Complete Project	Grading Rubric	Explanation

Matrix Components

American Short Stories: 1920 to the Present 25

    Table of Contents 25

    Essential Selections 27

    Teaching and Assessment Resources, Sample Pages 29

    Related Longer Works 43

Literature & Thought, The Harlem Renaissance 47

    Table of Contents 47

    Teacher Guide, Sample Pages 49

Literature & Thought, Times of Change: Vietnam and the 60s 50

    Table of Contents 50

    Teacher Guide, Sample Pages 52

The Essential Guide to Language, Writing, & Literature, Blue Level . . . 53

    Table of Contents 53

    Teacher Guide, Sample Pages 57

UNIT TWO

Literature from the 1950s and 1960s

THE VELDT (1950) RAY BRADBURY 169

BARN BURNING (1950) WILLIAM FAULKNER 185

ANGEL LEVINE (1955) BERNARD MALAMUD 207

THE WRYSONS (1978) JOHN CHEEVER 221

HARRISON BERGERON (1961) KURT VONNEGUT 231

EVERYTHING THAT RISES MUST CONVERGE (1961)
FLANNERY O'CONNOR 241

A & P (1961) JOHN UPDIKE 259

THE SKY IS GRAY (1963) ERNEST J. GAINES 269

THE WOOING OF ARIADNE (1965) HARRY MARK PETRAKIS 299

Responding to Unit Two 314

TO THE READER 8
ON STYLE 10
LITERARY ELEMENTS OF THE SHORT STORY 13

UNIT ONE

Literature from the 1920s to the 1940s

IN ANOTHER COUNTRY (1927) ERNEST HEMINGWAY 21

HE (1930) KATHERINE ANNE PORTER 29

BABYLON REVISITED (1931) F. SCOTT FITZGERALD 43

THE FAR AND THE NEAR (1935) THOMAS WOLFE 67

SUCKER (1936) CARSON MCCULLERS 73

THE CHRYSANTHEMUMS (1937) JOHN STEINBECK 85

WHY I LIVE AT THE P.O. (1941) EUDORA WELTY 99

THE BLACK BALL (ca. 1941) RALPH ELLISON 115

THE SECRET LIFE OF WALTER MITTY (1942) JAMES THURBER 127

THE LOTTERY (1944) SHIRLEY JACKSON 135

MIRIAM (1945) TRUMAN CAPOTE 147

Responding to Unit One 162

UNIT THREE

Literature from the 1970s and 1980s

THE KEY (1970) ISAAC BASHEVIS SINGER   321
THE FLOWERS (1973) ALICE WALKER   333
WHERE HAVE YOU GONE, CHARMING BILLY? (1975) TIM O'BRIEN   337
EVERYTHING STUCK TO HIM (1981) RAYMOND CARVER   349
DETROIT SKYLINE, 1949 (1982) BOBBIE ANN MASON   357
AMERICAN HORSE (1983) LOUISE ERDRICH   377
THE WRITER IN THE FAMILY (1984) E.L. DOCTOROW   391
THE FISH (1986) RUSSELL BANKS   407
TRUCKSTOP (1987) GARRISON KEILLOR   417
RULES OF THE GAME (1989) AMY TAN   425

Responding to Unit Three   438

UNIT FOUR

Literature from the 1990s

LADIES AND GENTLEMEN: (1990) JOYCE CAROL OATES   445
FAULT LINES (1992) BARBARA KINGSOLVER   455
TOP OF THE FOOD CHAIN (1992) T. CORAGHESSAN BOYLE   467
LETTERS FROM MY FATHER (1992) ROBERT OLEN BUTLER   475
THIS IS WHAT IT MEANS TO SAY PHOENIX, ARIZONA (1993)
   SHERMAN ALEXIE   485
THE INTRUDER (1995) ANDRE DUBUS   499
MORTALS (1996) TOBIAS WOLFF   513
CHARLIE HOGLE'S EARRING (1997) PAUL THEROUX   525

Responding to Unit Four   540

GLOSSARY OF LITERARY TERMS   542
INDEX OF TITLES AND AUTHORS   546

American Short Stories: **Essential Selections**

When time and/or ability level do not allow for teaching an entire unit, you may find the following list helpful. The most representative selections in each unit are noted, along with their difficulty levels. Teaching these selections will give students the essence of the unit.

UNIT ONE: LITERATURE FROM THE 1920s TO THE 1940s

In Another Country by Ernest Hemingway, page 21, *Easy*

He by Katherine Anne Porter, page 29, *Average*

Babylon Revisited by F. Scott Fitzgerald, page 43, *Challenging*

The Far and the Near by Thomas Wolfe, page 67, *Average*

Sucker by Carson McCullers, page 73, *Easy*

The Chrysanthemums by John Steinbeck, page 85, *Average*

The Black Ball by Ralph Ellison, page 115, *Average*

The Secret Life of Walter Mitty by James Thurber, page 127, *Easy*

UNIT TWO: LITERATURE FROM THE 1950s AND 1960s

The Veldt by Ray Bradbury, page 169, *Easy*

Barn Burning by William Faulkner, page 185, *Challenging*

Angel Levine by Bernard Malamud, page 207, *Average*

The Wrysons by John Cheever, page 221, *Average*

Harrison Bergeron by Kurt Vonnegut, page 231, *Average*

A & P by John Updike, page 259, *Easy*

The Sky Is Gray by Ernest J. Gaines, page 269, *Average*

The Wooing of Ariadne by Harry Mark Petrakis, page 299, *Easy*

UNIT THREE: LITERATURE FROM THE 1970s AND 1980s

The Key by Isaac Bashevis Singer, page 321, *Average*

The Flowers by Alice Walker, page 333, *Average*

Where Have You Gone, Charming Billy? by Tim O'Brien, page 337, *Challenging*

Detroit Skyline, 1949 by Bobbie Ann Mason, page 357, *Easy*

American Horse by Louise Erdrich, page 377, *Average*

The Writer in the Family by E.L. Doctorow, page 391, *Average*

Truckstop by Garrison Keillor, page 417, *Easy*

Rules of the Game by Amy Tan, page 425, *Average*

UNIT FOUR: LITERATURE FROM THE 1990s

Ladies and Gentlemen: by Joyce Carol Oates, page 445, *Easy*

Fault Lines by Barbara Kingsolver, page 455, *Average*

Top of the Food Chain by T. Coraghessan Boyle, page 467, *Average*

Letters from My Father by Robert Olen Butler, page 475, *Easy*

This Is What It Means to Say Phoenix, Arizona by Sherman Alexie, page 485, *Easy*

The Intruder by Andre Dubus, page 499, *Average*

Mortals by Tobias Wolff, page 513, *Average*

Charlie Hogle's Earring by Paul Theroux, page 525, *Average*

Active Reading Strategies

Active Reading means being an interested and focused reader. It involves thinking about what what you are going to read, what you are reading, and what you have just read. Use the information below to become an active reader.

Pre-Reading

Before you even begin reading, ask yourself, "Why am I reading this? What do I hope to learn from it?" Look at the title, and think about what it might tell you about the text. Skim over the pages, looking for subheadings, captions, sidebars, or illustrations that give you clues about what you are going to read.

During Reading

If you own the book you are reading, you should highlight, underline, and annotate as you read. This emphasizes the information and helps transmit it to your brain. You can also easily review these important points later. Always be sure to monitor your reading by constantly mulling over the information, images, impressions, and so on that you are receiving from the text. The best way to do this is to use the six Active Reading strategies outlined below. The more you employ these strategies, the more help they will offer. They should become second nature to you.

- **Questioning**

  Ask questions that come to mind as you read.

  Continually questioning the text will help you stay alert and interested in what you are reading. As your questions are answered, think of new ones.

- **Predicting**

  Use what has happened to guess what will happen next.

  As you read, keep guessing as to what will happen next. Think about what the characters are up to, where the plot is going, and what the author will do next. Keep making predictions right up to the end of the reading.

- **Clarifying**

  Clear up any confusion about the text and resolve any questions.

  If you have trouble understanding something you have read, clear it up right away. Go back and reread the passage until you understand it. Think about the main idea of the passage. Continually clarify what the author is telling you throughout your reading.

- **Connecting**

  Compare the text with your own experience.

  Connect what you read to something you have read, seen, or experienced yourself. Ask yourself, "What does this remind me of?" Visualize the information—try to see it in your mind. When you connect with the characters and situations you read about, your reading is more meaningful.

- **Summarizing**

  Review what has happened so far.

  Every now and again as you read, stop to review what you have read so far. Determine what you know, what you think you know, and what has changed about what you thought you knew.

- **Evaluating**

  Form opinions and arrive at conclusions about your reading.

  Make judgments as you read. Use your common sense as well as the evidence in the text to arrive at sound opinions and valid conclusions.

After Reading

When you finish reading, stop to think about what you have read. Go over the entire piece in your head. Try to remember the main points and the relevant details. Use a response journal to jot down your feelings about what you've read.

Active Reading Model

The Flowers

Alice Walker

It seemed to Myop as she skipped lightly from hen house to pigpen to smokehouse that the days had never been as beautiful as these. The air held a keenness that made her nose twitch. The harvesting of the corn and cotton, peanuts and squash, made each day a golden surprise that caused excited little tremors to run up her jaws.

Myop carried a short, knobby stick. She struck out at random at chickens she liked, and worked out the beat of a song on the fence around the pigpen. She felt light and good in the warm sun. She was ten, and nothing existed for her but her song, the stick clutched in her dark brown hand, and the tat-de-ta-ta-ta of accompaniment.

Turning her back on the rusty boards of her family's sharecropper cabin, Myop walked along the fence till it ran into the stream made by the spring. Around the spring, where the family got drinking water, silver ferns and wildflowers grew. Along the shallow banks pigs rooted. Myop watched the tiny white bubbles disrupt the thin black scale of soil and the water that silently rose and slid away down the stream.

She had explored the woods behind the house many times. Often, in late autumn, her mother took her to gather nuts among the fallen leaves. Today she made her own path, bouncing this way and that way, vaguely keeping an eye out for snakes. She found, in addition to various common but pretty ferns and leaves, an armful of strange blue flowers with velvety ridges and a sweetsuds bush full of the brown, fragrant buds.

By twelve o'clock, her arms laden with sprigs of her findings, she was a mile or more from home. She had often been as far before, but the strangeness of the land made it not as pleasant as her usual haunts. It seemed gloomy in the little cove in which she found herself. The air was damp, the silence close and deep.

Questioning: I wonder who Myop is? Does she live on a farm? What time period is this? What kind of a name is Myop?

Connecting: I remember exploring the woods near Grandpa's house last summer.

Predicting: The story is beginning to sound more ominous. Maybe she'll get lost.

Myop began to circle back to the house, back to the peacefulness of the morning. It was then she stepped smack into his eyes. Her heel became lodged in the broken ridge between brow and nose, and she reached down quickly, unafraid, to free herself. It was only when she saw his naked grin that she gave a little yelp of surprise.

He had been a tall man. From feet to neck covered a long space. His head lay beside him. When she pushed back the leaves and layers of earth and debris Myop saw that he'd had large white teeth, all of them cracked or broken, long fingers, and very big bones. All his clothes had rotted away except some threads of blue denim from his overalls. The buckles of the overalls had turned green.

Myop gazed around the spot with interest. Very near where she'd stepped into the head was a wild pink rose. As she picked it to add to her bundle she noticed a raised mound, a ring, around the rose's root. It was the rotted remains of a noose, a bit of shredding plowline, now blending benignly into the soil. Around an overhanging limb of a great spreading oak clung another piece. Frayed, rotted, bleached, and frazzled—barely there—but spinning restlessly in the breeze. Myop laid down her flowers.

And the summer was over.

Clarifying: Wait—what did she step on? It must be a skull!

Summarizing: Myop was walking in the woods and found the corpse of a man who's been dead for awhile.

Evaluating: Myop will never be the same. Not only is the summer over—her childhood is over.

Name _____ Class _____ Date _____

Active Reading Practice

The Far and the Near

Thomas Wolfe

As you read the short story that follows, use the Active Reading strategies to better understand and appreciate the story. Answer the questions and then continue using the strategies on the lines provided. Mark the text in any way you find helpful.

On the outskirts of a little town upon a rise of land that swept back from the railway there was a tidy little cottage of white boards, trimmed vividly with green blinds. To one side of the house there was a garden neatly patterned with plots of growing vegetables, and an arbor for the grapes which ripened late in August. Before the house there were three mighty oaks which sheltered it in their clean and massive shade in summer, and to the other side there was a border of gay flowers. The whole place had an air of tidiness, thrift, and modest comfort.

Every day, a few minutes after two o'clock in the afternoon, the limited express between two cities passed this spot. At that moment the great train, having halted for a breathing-space at the town near by, was beginning to lengthen evenly into its stroke, but it had not yet reached the full drive of its terrific speed. It swung into view deliberately, swept past with a powerful swaying motion of the engine, a low smooth rumble of its heavy cars upon pressed steel, and then it vanished in the cut. For a moment the progress of the engine could be marked by heavy bellowing puffs of smoke that burst at spaced intervals above the edges of the meadow grass, and finally nothing could be heard but the solid clacking tempo of the wheels receding into the drowsy stillness of the afternoon.

Every day for more than twenty years, as the train had approached this house, the engineer had blown on the whistle, and every day, as soon as she heard this signal, a woman had appeared on the back porch of the little house and waved to him. At first she had a small child clinging to her skirts, and now this child had grown to full

Questions: Who do you think lives in this "tidy" house?
_____
_____
_____

26 © Perfection Learning Corporation • REPRODUCIBLE

Many Voices: American Short Stories

---

womanhood, and every day she, too, came with her mother to the porch and waved.

The engineer had grown old and gray in service. He had driven his great train, loaded with its weight of lives, across the land ten thousand times. His own children had grown up and married, and four times he had seen before him on the tracks the ghastly dot of tragedy converging like a cannon ball to its eclipse of horror at the boiler head—a light spring wagon filled with children, with its clustered row of small stunned faces; a cheap automobile stalled upon the tracks, set with the wooden figures of people paralyzed with fear; a battered hobo walking by the rail, too deaf and old to hear the whistle's warning; and a form flung past his window with a scream—all this the man had seen and known. He had known all the grief, the joy, the peril and the labor such a man could know; he had grown seamed and weathered in his loyal service, and now, schooled by the qualities of faith and courage and humbleness that attended his labor, he had grown old, and had the grandeur and the wisdom these men have.

But no matter what peril or tragedy he had known, the vision of the little house and the women waving to him with a brave free motion of the arm had become fixed in the mind of the engineer as something beautiful and enduring, something beyond all change and ruin, and something that would always be the same, no matter what mishap, grief or error might break the iron schedule of his days.

The sight of the little house and of these two women gave him the most extraordinary happiness he had ever known. He had seen them in a thousand lights, a hundred weathers. He had seen them through the harsh bare light of wintry gray across the brown and frosted stubble of the earth, and he had seen them again in the green luring sorcery of April.

He felt for them and for the little house in which they lived such tenderness as a man might feel for his own children, and at length the picture of their lives was carved so sharply in his heart that he felt

Clarifying: What do the image of the house and the women mean to the engineer?
_____

Many Voices: American Short Stories © Perfection Learning Corporation • REPRODUCIBLE 27

Differentiated Instruction

Unit One: Literature from the 1920s to the 1940s

Discuss with students the overview of American history from 1920 to 1950 on pages 18–19 of the student book. Also, ask them to contribute any information they might have about the subject matter of the photographs on these pages as well as those on pages 16–17. To set the mood for the selections, play recordings of popular music from this time period, such as the music of Louis Armstrong, Glenn Miller, and Duke Ellington.

Differentiated Classroom Tip:

With a longer, more difficult selection, arrange students into groups of five or so, mixing their learning styles and abilities. Assign each one a different aspect of the selection to investigate, for example, theme, plot, character motivation, setting, or viewpoint. Each member of the group researches the assignment at his or her own reading level. Then groups split up so that all students investigating the same aspect compare notes and teach one another. Finally, students return to their original groups so that every member of each group can report to the others and share their knowledge.

Name of Selection	TYPE OF LEARNER			
	Auditory	Visual	Kinesthetic	ELL/Struggling
In Another Country pp. 21–27 Easy	Have students read the story aloud to one another. Encourage discussion as they read.	Ask students to draw or paint a view of 1940s Milan, based on the descriptions in the first few paragraphs of the story.	Have students try to recreate the exercises the soldiers were asked to perform with the machines at the hospital.	Help students interpret the meaning of the story by focusing on the significance of the major's words, "I am utterly unable to resign myself."
He pp. 29–41 Average	Assign two students the roles of Mr. and Mrs. Whipple. Have them read aloud the dialogue between the two characters on p. 30 and on p. 32.	Have students draw a portrait of Mrs. Whipple.	Have students pantomime His movements when He was leading the bull home to the barn.	Discuss with students Mrs. Whipple's conflicting emotions. Why did she begin to cry in the final scene of the story?
Babylon Revisited pp. 43–65 Challenging	Assign students the roles of Charlie, Marion, and Lincoln. Have them act out the scene in part III of the story.	Show students photos of Paris landmarks mentioned in the story, such as Montmartre and the opera house.	Assign two students the roles of Marion and Lincoln. Assign another two students the roles of Lorraine and Duncan. Have the students use their facial expressions, body language, and tone of voice to demonstrate the contrast between the two couples.	Discuss with the students the reasons why Marion does not want to let Honoria live with Charlie.

What Do You Know?

(Prior Knowledge Guide)

You are about to begin reading a book of American short stories from 1920 to the present. This is not a test, but a way to find out what you already think, feel, and know.

1. Do you prefer reading stories, novels, nonfiction, or poetry? Explain why.
2. If you were writing a definition of a short story for a dictionary, what would it be?
3. In what ways do you think stories that were written in the first half of the 20th century might be different from those written in recent years?
4. In what ways do you think they might be similar?
5. Who are the famous writers of the 20th century? List as many as you can.
6. Do you know anything about any of these writers? If so, what do you know or think you might know?
7. What does "style" mean in writing?
8. Tell who one of your favorite writers is and describe her or his style.
9. What elements might go into creating a writer's style?
10. Does your own writing have a voice that is uniquely yours? If so, how would you describe it?

AMERICAN SHORT STORIES TEACHING AND ASSESSMENT RESOURCES, SAMPLE PAGES

Name _____ Class _____ Date _____

Unit One Vocabulary

Watch for the following words as you read the selections in Unit One. Record your own vocabulary words and definitions on the blank lines.

In Another Country pages 21–26

pavilions annexes; outbuildings

_____

_____

He pages 29–40

mortally intensely; unremittingly
vittles food

_____

_____

Babylon Revisited pages 43–64

antipathy intense dislike
bourgeois middle-class; conventional
buxom full-figured
chastened humble; disciplined
colloquial familiar; ordinary
conciliate soothe; appease
equanimity pleasant calmness
expostulation justification
feigned pretended
ferreted searched
irrevocably permanently; unchangeably
judicially critically; with judgment
modulated adjusted; modified
monosyllables one-syllable words
nicely correctness; propriety
piquant charming
portentous ominous; full of meaning
provocative suggestive; exciting
recalcitrant difficult to manage
reproof criticism; reprimand

restiveness uneasiness
roguishly mischievously
sinister dangerous looking
strident commanding attention
sustenance nourishment; support
tepid lukewarm; unenthusiastic
tranquility calmly
vehemently forcefully; with conviction

_____

_____

The Far and the Near pages 67–70

sorcery magic
timorous fearful
vista view

_____

_____

Sucker pages 73–82

_____

_____

_____

_____

continued

© Perfection Learning Corporation • Reproducible

Many Voices: American Short Stories 33

Name of Selection	TYPE OF LEARNER			
	Auditory	Visual	Kinesthetic	ELL/Struggling
The Far and the Near pp. 67-71 Average	Have pairs of students read the story aloud to each other. One student reads the first part of the story and the second student reads the part that begins, "That day came."	Have students sketch or paint a landscape showing the view of the house from the train.	Have students act out the scene when the engineer visits the house and the woman answers the door.	Discuss with the students the meaning of the story. How was the engineer changed by his experience visiting the house?
Sucker pp. 73-83 Easy	Have students retell the story from Sucker's point of view.	Have students create a drawing or painting of Pete and Sucker's room.	Have students try to demonstrate "the look of a person who is surprised and expecting something swell."	Discuss with students the relationship between the narrator and Sucker. Why couldn't they go back to the way things used to be?
The Chrysanthemums pp. 85-97 Average	Assign to students the roles of the characters in the story. Read the narration of the story aloud to the class, allowing the students to speak the lines of dialogue.	Ask students to draw or work with clay to create an image inspired by the story.	Bring in a bouquet of chrysanthemums for students to touch and smell.	Help students sort through Elisa's words and actions for clues about what she is really feeling and thinking.
Why I Live at the P.O. pp. 99-113 Average	Assign to students the roles of the characters in the story. Have one student assigned to be Sister reads the story, allowing the students in the other roles to speak their lines of dialogue.	Ask students to imagine a stage production of the story. Have them design the scenery and costumes.	Have students take turns demonstrating the body language of one of the characters. Have the other students guess which character they are demonstrating.	Explain to students the concept of an "unreliable narrator."
The Black Ball pp. 115-125 Average	Have students describe what happens in the story and read the most significant passages aloud.	Have students create an illustration depicting a scene from the story, using only the colors black, white, and brown.	Bring in a black ball. Have students toss the ball to each other as they discuss the symbolism of the ball in the story.	Help students understand the risks the narrator might have faced if he joined a union or even attended a union meeting.
The Secret Life of Walter Mitty pp. 127-133 Easy	Have pairs of students read the story aloud to each other. One student reads the fantasy sections and one student reads the narration.	Have students create a four-panel comic strip based on one of Mitty's imaginary adventures.	Have students act out one of Mitty's imaginary adventures.	Have students identify the elements from Mitty's ordinary life that inspire his fantasies.
The Lottery pp. 135-145 Easy	Have students read the story aloud to one another. Encourage them to identify clues that foreshadow the dark ending of the story.	Have students paint or sketch a landscape that represents the setting of the story.	Assign roles and act out the story, using folded slips of paper as props.	Discuss with students why some readers have been outraged by this story.
Miriam pp. 147-160 Challenging	Have students describe what happens in the story and read aloud the passages when Miriam appears.	Have students draw a portrait of Miriam.	Have students act out the scene when Miriam arrives with her box and her doll.	Help students understand that the meaning of the story is deliberately ambiguous. Discuss their ideas for the meaning of the story.

32 Literature from the 1920s to the 1940s

Many Voices: American Short Stories

Name _____ Class _____ Date _____

The Chrysanthemums pages 85–96

ambassadorial formal; diplomatic
asperity roughness
fawning cringing
skirling making a shrill sound
tamped packed tightly

_____
_____

Why I Live at the P. O. pages 99–112

disport frolic; play around
piecing picking at; snacking on
precarious uncertain; dangerous
prostrated exhausted; flattened

_____
_____
_____

The Black Ball pages 115–124

_____
_____
_____
_____
_____

The Secret Life of Walter Mitty pages 127–132

craven cowardly; contemptible

_____
_____

The Lottery pages 135–144

interminably endlessly

_____
_____
_____

Miriam pages 147–160

skein loose coil, as of thread or yarn

_____
_____

In Another Country by Ernest Hemingway, pages 21–26   1927

Summary

In a reserved and matter-of-fact tone, an American recounts his experiences in Italy during World War I as he undergoes physical therapy to treat war wounds.

Vocabulary

pavilions annexes; outbuildings

Responding to the Story

1. *Literary Lens* Mood is conveyed through descriptions of the setting, the author's (or narrator's) attitude toward the story, and through imagery. Select one of the images in the story and describe how it influences the mood of the story. *Several images establish a mood of emptiness and loss: the deer hanging in front of the shops "stiff and heavy and empty," the machines that unfeelingly administer physical therapy; the major refusing to look at the pictures of healthy hands but staring out the "empty" window.*

2. Hemingway once defined courage as "grace under pressure." In what way, if at all, is this idea demonstrated in "In Another Country"? *Students may note that the major faces the loss of his wife and his fencing hand with courage. Also, "carrying himself straight and soldierly, with tears on both cheeks and biting his lips, he walked past the machines and out the door."*

3. Hemingway is known as an "existentialist" writer. Existentialism is the belief that humans exist in an empty universe that does not care about human existence. In the face of this nothingness and loneliness, humans must create their own meaning and purpose. In what ways does "In Another Country" reflect the idea of existentialism? *Answers will vary. Help students to see how the following reflect existentialism.*

   The war: The war appears pointless, distant, and cold.

   The machines: The machines are also metaphors. They act automatically and have no consideration for those they are "helping."

   The major: The major is the ultimate existentialist. He faces the future with courage despite losing everything meaningful.*

   The hawks: The soldiers fend off sorrows by finding meaning in their medals and accepting the purposes of the war. The existentialist goes beyond these trappings of meaning and faces the true meaninglessness of existence.*

4. What do you think the view of the narrator is toward the war and the military establishment? Support your answer with evidence from the text. *Students may note that the narrator's discussion of medals and his skepticism about the machinery show that he questions the value and meaning of war.*

5. *The Author's Style* After reading the quotation below, locate two sentences in the story that seem to fit his description of the "true simple declarative sentence."

   One True Sentence

   Sometimes when I was starting a new story and I could not get it going . . . . I would stand and look out over the roofs of Paris and think, "Do not worry. You have always written before and you will write now. All you have to do is write one true sentence. Write the truest sentence that you know." So finally I would write one true sentence, and then go on from there . . . . If I started to write elaborately, or like someone introducing or presenting something, I found that I could cut that scrollwork or ornament out and throw it away and start with the first true simple declarative sentence I had written.

   —Ernest Hemingway, *A Moveable Feast*

   Answers will vary. Examples of simple declarative sentences are

   • *page 21: It was cold in the fall in Milan and the dark came very early.*
   • *page 23: He had lived a very long time with death and was a little detached.*
   • *page 26: The photographs did not make much difference to the major because he only looked out of the window.*

Name _____ Class _____ Date _____

In Another Country by Ernest Hemingway, pages 21–26

Skill Development: Recognize Tone

A story's tone refers to the author or narrator's attitude toward the subject of a work. An author might have an ironic, humorous, or serious tone, to name a few. In the story "In Another Country," Hemingway communicates the tone of the story through techniques such as diction (word choice) and descriptive language.

Directions: Use the web below to examine the tone of the story "In Another Country." In the center of the web, write in your own words a sentence or phrase that describes the tone of the story. In the circles surrounding the center, write short quotes from the story that demonstrate the tone.

Quote / Tone / Quote / Quote / Quote

Many Voices: American Short Stories

© Perfection Learning Corporation • Reproducible   37

Name _____ Class _____ Date _____

In Another Country by Ernest Hemingway, pages 21–26

Comprehension Quiz

Choose the best answer and write the letter on the blank.

____ 1. The story takes place in—
A. Rome.
B. Scala.
C. Little Italy.
D. Milan.

____ 2. The narrator injured his—
A. hand.
B. face.
C. leg.
D. arm.

____ 3. The _____ did not "have confidence."
A. narrator
B. doctor
C. major
D. tall boy

____ 4. The narrator was not—
A. an officer.
B. a soldier.
C. an American.
D. a hawk.

____ 5. The major said a man must not—
A. fight.
B. marry.
C. cry.
D. lose.

6. In what ways does the narrator see himself as different from the other wounded soldiers who visit the hospital?

_____

_____

_____

7. What did the major mean when he said, "I am utterly unable to resign myself"? What do you think Hemingway was trying to communicate to the reader when he wrote this scene?

_____

_____

_____

36   © Perfection Learning Corporation • Reproducible   **Many Voices: American Short Stories**

He by Katherine Anne Porter, pages 29–40   1930

Summary
The Whipples, a poor farming family, struggle to make ends meet during hard times. Mrs. Whipple's obsessions with her disabled son and with other people's opinions create tensions in the family, which escalate when the Whipples are forced to place the boy in an institution.

Vocabulary
mortally intensely; unremittingly
vittles food

Responding to the Story
1. **Literary Lens** Define what you think is the major conflict in this short story. Answers may vary. *There are several conflicts in the story, including the Whipple's struggle to provide for their family and Mrs. Whipple's ongoing battle to prove to the neighbors that He is well cared for. But the major conflict seems to be between Mr. and Mrs. Whipple, who are constantly at odds and often critical of each other due to the worries and demands of caring for a disabled child in the midst of poverty.*

2. Why do you think the other members of the family in this story refer to the mentally disabled boy as "He"? Answers may vary. *The fact that they don't think of him as a complete, valuable individual. His inability to communicate and passive behavior seem to relegate him to a protected but inferior position in the family, unworthy of the distinction of his own name. "He" becomes more of a symbol of the family's hardships than a person in his own right.*

3. Do you think Mrs. Whipple failed her son in any way? If so, what could she have done differently? Answers will vary. Some students may note that *Mrs. Whipple defended her son from the disparaging words of others, and gave up her own blanket to warm him when he was ill. Others may point out that she had him do dangerous things, and that she "boxed his ears" for getting dirty when she wanted him clean. Because he didn't speak or seem to understand, his parents didn't explain things to him,*

so he didn't understand being sent away. There is no right answer. Encourage the class to empathize with both the disabled son and with Mrs. Whipple in her obvious guilt and anguish at his condition, her daily frustrations over him, and her efforts in a difficult situation.

4. Do you think that attitudes toward mentally disabled people have changed very much since this story was written? Explain. *This question doesn't necessarily have an answer, but is designed to make students think. Encourage open discussion. Students may observe that mentally disabled people have more diagnostic, treatment, and assistance options available now than the story indicated, and that it would be less acceptable now to express the view that it would be "A Lord's mercy if He should die" or that his disability was the result of "the sins of the fathers." But the mixed responses of covert pity and judgment masked by apparent acceptance and optimism are still apparent today.*

5. **The Author's Style** Porter is known for her ability to bring complex characters to life. Select a passage that you think demonstrates Porter's skill at characterization. Be prepared to explain your choice. An example of an appropriate passage is paragraph six of the story, which reveals in a few sentences Mrs. Whipple's complex combination of denial, obsession, and defensiveness about her son's disability; her love for him and championing of his particular abilities; and her desperate need for reassurance and comfort.

Name _____ Class _____ Date _____

He by Katherine Anne Porter, pages 29–40

Comprehension Quiz
Choose the best answer and write the letter on the blank.

_____ 1. When anybody set foot in the house, the subject of _____ always came up.
A. money
B. farming
C. He
D. Mrs. Whipple

_____ 2. The preacher said He didn't get hurt because He was—
A. strong.
B. innocent.
C. simple.
D. fat.

_____ 3. When Mrs. Whipple was thinking, her _____ moved.
A. hands
B. eyes
C. head
D. lips

_____ 4. The doctor said He isn't as _____ as He looks.
A. stout
B. sick
C. young
D. simple

_____ 5. The neighbor who drove them to the County Home didn't dare—
A. speak the truth.
B. drive too fast.
C. look behind him.
D. ask for money.

6. What do you think Mrs. Whipple's brother meant when he wrote, "Put the big pot in the little one"?

7. What similarities can you find between the incident when He caught the pig and the incident when He fetched the bull? What do you think the author was trying to communicate with these scenes?

RESPONDING TO UNIT ONE

Literature from the 1920s to the 1940s

1. For their grotesque and macabre incidents, both "The Lottery" and "Miriam" might appear in a collection of horror stories. Which do you find more satisfyingly creepy and why? Answers will vary. The horror is more blatant in "The Lottery," but some students may be put off by the shocking brutality of the story; and find the skillful creepiness of "Miriam" easier to appreciate.

2. Reread the last paragraph of each story in this unit. Which do you think is the most memorable and why? Answers will vary. Many of the stories have memorable final paragraphs. For sheer shock value, some students might vote for "The Lottery" or "Miriam." The ending of "The Secret Life of Walter Mitty" is both amusing and thought-provoking. The final paragraphs of both "Sucker" and "The Far and the Near" are memorable for the sad and lasting impact of each story's events on the narrator. And the final paragraph of "The Black Ball" stands out as the only example of a hopeful ending.

3. In three of the stories in this unit—"He," "The Far and the Near," and "The Chrysanthemums"—at least one important character is never given a name. Why do you think the author made this choice in each instance? Answers may vary. In "He," as explored on the selection page, the author conveys the attitude of family members and neighbors that the mentally disabled boy is somehow less than a full person, not quite worthy of his own name. None of the characters in "The Far and the Near" are given a name. It helps the reader to get the message if we see the engineer as a symbol of "everyman" rather than as a distinct individual, and it is easier for the engineer to project his own wishes onto the lives of the women if he sees them in the abstract rather than as real people. Perhaps the fixer in "The Chrysanthemums" remains nameless because it is the mystery and adventure that he and his life suggest to Elisa that attract her and cause her to behave uncharacteristically, questioning herself and her life, more than the man himself.

4. The theme of the mysterious stranger is common in literature. In the traditional form of this theme, a mysterious stranger appears in the life of an individual or community. In a series of dramatic events, the stranger makes a sacrifice through which the life of the individual or community is improved. Choose one of the short stories in this chapter that features a stranger: "The Chrysanthemums," "Miriam," or "The Black Ball." Explain how the story fits, or deviates from, the theme of the mysterious stranger. Answers will vary. In "The Chrysanthemums," the stranger makes no sacrifice and, in fact, lacks the selflessness implied in the concept of sacrifice for another's good. Yet his encounter with Elisa causes her to reevaluate herself and her life in a way that may, ultimately, help her grow and develop as a person. In "Miriam," the stranger is clearly not a benign, sacrificing presence and the source of growth or improvement for Mrs. Miller. Instead, she appears to signal a drastic and dangerous change in Mrs. Miller's life. Of the three stories mentioned, this one deviates furthest from the traditional theme of the mysterious stranger. The union organizer in "The Black Ball," by contrast, fits the theme well. He arrives as a stranger, offering dramatic evidence of his sacrifices for the causes of civil rights and fair labor practices, and offers John an opportunity that gives him hope that things can be better for him and his son.

5. The ball is important in "The Black Ball" and the black box plays a central role in "The Lottery." What do these two objects have in common? Answers may vary. Physically, both objects are small and black. The color of the box seems to symbolize the evil of the lottery ritual itself, in the classic "light equals good, dark equals evil" mode. The color of the ball in "The Black Ball" is a more complex symbol, standing for both race itself and the evils of "the game" of racial prejudice and discrimination. In both cases the item itself is relatively harmless: each is simply a tool for the corrupt social practices in which it is used.

6. The first six stories in this unit have a theme of loss in common. In your opinion, which story evokes the most pathos? Answers will vary. The major in "In Another Country" and the title character in "Sucker" claim the reader's compassion for they did not cause the pain that comes to them in the stories. While neither Charlie Wales in "Babylon Revisited" nor the Whipples in "He" are as sympathetic characters as the major in "Sucker," both demonstrate sincere effort in dealing with the problems in which they find themselves. The very "humanness" of the actions of the engineer in "The Far and the Near" may cause students who identify with their failings to respond with pity or compassion. And students prone to introspection and personal drive to achieve may empathize with Elisa in "The Chrysanthemums."

7. Hemingway and Fitzgerald were both friends and competitors, moving in the same social circles and writing during the same era. What differences and similarities do you see between "In Another Country" and "Babylon Revisited"? Answers will vary. Both stories are set in large European cities, though about 10 years apart, with World War II creating a larger gulf between the two settings than a more normal decade would indicate. Both have a cosmopolitan feeling and rather world-weary tone, based on the life experiences of the characters. Both deal with loss, as already pointed out. But the styles and messages are very different. In contrast to Hemingway's understated style, unglamorous plot and interest in the "true simple declarative sentence," Fitzgerald uses complex sentences and lively dialogue, language, and action to depict the excesses of a hedonistic lifestyle and their consequences carried into the present. And while neither story provides a happy ending for its characters, the bleakness of Hemingway's existentialist views creates a very different tone from the determined purposefulness of Fitzgerald's protagonist. While Hemingway's characters are largely "acted upon," and choose only how to react, Fitzgerald's characters actively pursue their goals with a sense of control and conviction.

8. The opening sentence of Anna Karenina by the Russian author Leo Tolstoy reads: "All happy families resemble one another; every unhappy family is unhappy in its own way." In what unique ways are the families in "He" and "Why I Live at the P. O." unhappy? Answers will vary. The combination of stresses that have worn down the Whipples in "He" is certainly unusual. In the absence of solutions, the family has responded by turning inward with complaints, bickering, and criticism. While trying to maintain a public image of irreproachable care for the disabled son, their finances have gone from bad to worse and their internal relationships have deteriorated until Mr. and Mrs. Whipple seem isolated in their own private misery. By contrast, the quarrels and problems of the family in "Why I Live at the P. O." seem ordinary, petty, and unnecessary. It seems that any family member could break the stubborn cycle of irritation, defensiveness, and grudge-holding to set an example of reason, forgiveness, and peacemaking. Yet no one does. Perhaps what is unique about this family's unhappiness is their determination to remain unhappy.

Writing About the Literature

Staying Power

The stories in this unit were all written more than 50 years ago. Write a persuasive essay about which story you think has best stood the test of time. You may want to use passages from the story as evidence. Consider what is timeless about the style, theme, or characters of the story you choose. *You might review with students the elements of persuasive writing:*

- *The goal is to convince the reader to agree*
- *State your opinion clearly*
- *Back it up with facts and evidence*
- *Explain why the reader should agree*
- *Use emotive words like "must," "should," and "ought"*
- *Maintain a calm, reasonable tone*

You might also encourage students to organize their thoughts about style, theme, and characters using a chart like the one below.

Style	Theme	Characters

Writing with Style

Choose one of these two assignments. *Students may need coaching on how to approach this assignment. You might offer several steps to help them analyze and mimic the author's style. For example, suggest that students reread the story carefully, focusing on elements of style, and then use a chart to clarify important elements before they begin to write. Style elements to consider in these stories include:*

- *Tone: What is the mood of the story and how does the author create and change the mood?*
- *Voice: Who tells the story and from what point of view? Is it first person? How does the narrator relate to the action? What feelings does the author want you to have toward the narrator?*
- *Theme: What is the main message of the story? How can you convey a similar message in your composition?*
- *Setting: What sets the story in time and place, and how important is setting to the story?*
- *Language and Dialogue: What specific words or phrases define characters and help establish the setting? How is dialogue used?*
- *Other Techniques: How does the author create the desired effect and convey the message of the story? How much does the author rely on physical description? Does the author make use of sensory images, metaphor, etc., to emphasize the message?*

Sucker's Point of View Using Carson McCullers style, rewrite the climax of "Sucker" as an interior monologue from the point of view of Sucker.

"The Secret Life of _____ " Fill in the blank with the name of a seemingly ordinary character of your own creation. Using James Thurber's style, put this character into an everyday situation that the character converts into a grandiose fantasy starring him- or herself.

UNIT ONE

In Your Own Style

After reflecting on how important the theme of loss is in many of the stories in this unit, consider your own life. What have you or someone you know either already lost or would most hate to lose? Write about this in your own style. Choose between taking a nonfiction approach or using your own or others' experiences as a starting point for fiction. *In assigning writing that might produce self-revealing compositions, you might want to promise students that you will not share their work with the class without permission. You might suggest that students approach this assignment by creating a worksheet for themselves made up of questions to consider before they write. Questions like these might be useful:*

- *What kinds of losses did characters face in the stories from Unit One?*
- *What loss that you or someone you know faced will you write about?*
- *What happened? What were the events leading up to the loss?*
- *What are the important emotions surrounding the loss? (i.e. grief, anger, blame, depression, guilt, resentment, alienation from others, relief)*
- *Who felt those emotions and how were they expressed?*
- *What happened as a result of the loss? Were there long-term negative outcomes? Were there positive outcomes?*
- *Will your composition be fiction or nonfiction?*
- *Will you present a small incident related to the loss, or an overview of the experience?*
- *In what voice, or from what point of view, will you write?*
- *Will you use other characters besides the narrator to help tell the story? If so, whom?*

Name _____ Class _____ Date _____

Unit One Tests

pages 17–161

I. Vocabulary

Choose the meaning of the bold word in each passage.

1. Beyond the old hospital were the new brick pavilions, and there we met every afternoon and were all very polite and interested in what was the matter, and sat in the machines that were to make so much difference. ("In Another Country," p. 22)
Ⓐ walkways   Ⓒ outbuildings
Ⓑ clinics   Ⓓ studios

2. But the stillness in the Ritz bar was strange and **portentous**. ("Babylon Revisited," p. 44)
Ⓐ ominous   Ⓒ mischievous
Ⓑ meaningless   Ⓓ upsetting

3. He greeted Marion with his voice pitched carefully to avoid either feigned enthusiasm or dislike, but her response was more frankly **tepid**, though she minimized her expression of unalterable distrust by directing her regard toward his child. ("Babylon Revisited," p. 46)
Ⓐ lukewarm   Ⓒ angry
Ⓑ skeptical   Ⓓ resentful

4. It would last an hour or two hours, and it would be difficult, but if he modulated his inevitable resentment to the **chastened** attitude of the reformed sinner, he might win his point in the end. ("Babylon Revisited," p. 54)
Ⓐ righteous   Ⓒ cheerful
Ⓑ confident   Ⓓ humble

5. This was more difficult that he expected: he wanted to launch into a long **expostulation** and explanation, but he only said: "The night I locked her out— and she interrupted, "I don't feel up to going over that again." ("Babylon Revisited," p. 55)
Ⓐ sermon   Ⓒ argument
Ⓑ justification   Ⓓ tirade

6. At five he took a taxi and bought presents for all the Peters—a **piquant** cloth doll, a box of Roman soldiers, flowers for Marion, big linen handkerchiefs for Lincoln. ("Babylon Revisited," p. 60)
Ⓐ charming   Ⓒ tight-weave fabric
Ⓑ tiny   Ⓓ brightly colored

7. Duncan wagged his finger **roguishly** at Charlie. ("Babylon Revisited," p. 61)
Ⓐ angrily   Ⓒ mischievously
Ⓑ accusingly   Ⓓ threateningly

8. "Good night, sweetheart," he said vaguely, and then trying to make his voice more tender, trying to **conciliate** something, "Good night, dear children." ("Babylon Revisited," p. 63)
Ⓐ appease   Ⓒ extract
Ⓑ remember   Ⓓ ascertain

9. Then, for a brief agony of time, the man sat in an ugly little parlor, and he tried to talk while the two women stared at him with a dull, bewildered hostility, a sullen, **timorous** restraint. ("The Far and the Near," p. 70)
Ⓐ violent   Ⓒ fearful
Ⓑ insane   Ⓓ resentful

10. It turned into the farm road in front of her house, crooked old wheels **skirling** and squeaking. ("The Chrysanthemums," p. 88)
Ⓐ bouncing   Ⓒ wobbling
Ⓑ shrieking   Ⓓ dragging

Name _____ Class _____ Date _____

11. "Do you think it wise to **disport** with ketchup in Stella-Rondo's flesh-colored kimono?" ("Why I Live at the P. O.," p. 106)
Ⓐ paint   Ⓒ juggle
Ⓑ cook   Ⓓ frolic

12. Mitty looked at him and at the **craven** figure of Benbow, who drank, and at the grave uncertain faces of the two great specialists. ("The Secret Life of Walter Mitty," p. 129)
Ⓐ staggering   Ⓒ contemptible
Ⓑ comic   Ⓓ grotesque

II. Reading

Read the following passage from "He" by Katherine Anne Porter and answer the questions.

1 This didn't keep the neighbors from talking plainly among themselves. "A Lord's pure mercy if He
2 should die," they said. "It's the sins of the fathers," they agreed among themselves. "There's bad blood
3 and bad doings somewhere, you can bet on that." This behind the Whipples' backs. To their faces
4 everybody said, "He's not so bad off. He'll be all right yet. Look how He grows!"
5   Mrs. Whipple hated to talk about it, she tried to keep her mind off it, but every time anybody set
6 foot in the house, the subject always came up, and she had to talk about Him first, before she could
7 get on to anything else. It seemed to ease her mind. "I wouldn't have anything happen to Him for all
8 the world, but it just looks like I can't keep Him out of mischief. He's so strong and active, He's always
9 into everything; He was like that since He could walk. It's actually funny sometimes, the way He can
10 do anything, it's laughable to see Him up to His tricks. Emily has more accidents, I'm forever tying up
11 her bruises, and Adna can't fall a foot without cracking a bone. But He can do anything and not get a
12 scratch. The preacher said such a nice thing once when he was here. He said, and I'll remember it to
13 my dying day. The innocent walk with God—that's why He don't get hurt." Whenever Mrs. Whipple
14 repeated these words, she always felt a warm pool spread in her breast, and the tears would fill her eyes,
15 and then she could talk about something else.

___ 1. Paragraph 1 does not imply that the Whipples' neighbors are
a. hypocritical.
b. judgmental.
c. fearful.
d. superstitious.

___ 2. From lines 12–15 readers could infer that Mrs. Whipple is
a. religious.
b. sentimental.
c. in need of reassurance.
d. all of the above.

___ 3. Lines 7–11 offer an example of
a. neologism.
b. exaggeration.
c. vernacular.
d. personification.

___ 4. From paragraph 2, one might best characterize Mrs. Whipple's attitude toward her son as
a. tender.
b. worried.
c. defensive.
d. all of the above.

___ 5. This passage is an example of what narrative point of view?
a. first person
b. interior monologue
c. third person omniscient
d. third person

III. Essay

Select one of the prompts below and follow the directions.

Experiencing

Carefully reread the passage from "He" and write an essay explaining why you think Mrs. Whipple always talks about Him when company comes, even though she "hated to talk about it."

Interpreting

Carefully reread the passage, paying close attention to sentence structure. Write an essay describing Porter's use of simple, compound, and complex sentences and sentence fragments, and explain what the different types of sentences add to the story.

Evaluating

Porter uses this story to examine attitudes toward the mentally disabled at the time in which the story is set. Write an essay setting forth, in one sentence, what you think is the main message of the story. Support your opinion with references from the story.

IV. Reading

Read the following passage from "The Chrysanthemums" by John Steinbeck and answer the questions.

1   "It must be nice," she said. "It must be very nice. I wish women could do such things."
2   "It ain't the right kind of a life for a woman."
3   Her upper lip raised a little, showing her teeth. "How do you know? How can you tell?" she said.
4   "I don't know, ma'am," he protested. "Of course I don't know. Now here's your kettles, done. You
5 don't have to buy no new ones."
6   "How much?"
7   "Oh, fifty cents'll do. I keep my prices down and my work good. That's why I have all them satisfied
8 customers up and down the highway."
9   Elisa brought him a fifty-cent piece from the house and dropped it in his hand. "You might be
10 surprised to have a rival some time. I can sharpen scissors, too. And I can beat the dents out of little pots.
11 I could show you what a woman might do."
12   He put his hammer back in the oily box and shoved the little anvil out of sight. "It would be a lonely
13 life for a woman, ma'am, and a scarey life, too, with animals creeping under the wagon all night."
14   He climbed over the single-tree, steadying himself in the seat, picked up the lines. "Thank you kindly,
15 ma'am," he said. "I'll do like you told me; I'll go back and catch the Salinas road . . ." The wagon turned
16 and crawled out the entrance road and back the way it had come, along the river.
17   Elisa stood in front of her wire fence watching the slow progress of the caravan. Her shoulders were
18 straight, her head thrown back, her eyes half-closed, so that the scene came vaguely into them. Her
19 lips moved silently, forming the words, "Good-bye—good-bye." Then she whispered: "That's a bright
20 direction. There's a glowing there."

____ 1. This passage implies that women in Elisa's time and place were
   a. seen as weak and dependent.
   b. free to do whatever they chose.
   c. restricted to safe, traditional roles.
   d. easily fooled.

____ 2. Elisa's attitude in this passage can be best described as
   a. confident.
   b. wistful.
   c. challenging.
   d. all of the above.

____ 3. The fixer's comments offer an example of which of the following?
   a. vernacular
   b. satire
   c. parable
   d. subtle humor

____ 4. In line 17, the phrase "The wagon turned and crawled out the entrance road" is an example of
   a. fantasy.
   b. simile.
   c. unreliable narrator.
   d. personification.

____ 5. Line 3 describes a gesture in which Elisa's "upper lip raised a little, showing her teeth." Considering the context of the passage, this gesture might be best interpreted to show an attitude of
   a. shock.
   b. challenge.
   c. discouragement.
   d. relief.

V. Essay

Select one of the prompts below and follow the directions.

Experiencing

Imagine yourself as Elisa, and write an essay describing what your life is like 10 years after this story takes place.

Interpreting

At the end of the passage, Elisa whispers, "That's a bright direction. There's a glowing there." Write an essay explaining what you think Elisa means by those words. Support your explanation using references from the story.

Evaluating

Elisa's character expresses a universal longing to reach beyond our circumstances—to be more and do more. Find a character in another story from Unit One that shares Elisa's longing. For each character, explain how the author conveys this universal longing and makes the reader empathize with the character. How are the two characters similar and different? With which character do you feel the strongest empathy, and why?

Unit One Style Quiz

Based on what you've learned about the authors' styles, match each short story excerpt with its author from the box below.

_____ 1. He would never go to any more parties. Classical phrases played in his mind—that side of his life was closed, closed. Now when a man says "closed, closed" like that, you can be pretty sure that some woman has double-closed him, so to speak. Perry was also thinking that other classical thought, about how cowardly suicide is. A noble thought that one—warm and inspiring. Think of all the fine men we should lose if suicide were not so cowardly!

_____ 2. "Did you say Ellisville? That in the state of Mississippi?" Like lightning he had pulled out a red notebook entitled, "Permanent Facts & Data." He wrote down something. "I don't hear well."

Under "Ellis-Ville Miss" he was drawing a line; now he was flicking it with two little marks. "Maybe she didn't say she would. Maybe she said she wouldn't." He suddenly laughed very loudly, after the way he had whispered. Aimee jumped back. "Women!—Well, if we play anywheres near Ellisville, Miss., in the future I may look her up and I may not," he said.

_____ 3. With a high heart, because there was a unicorn in his garden, the man went upstairs and roused his wife again. "The unicorn," he said, "ate a lily." His wife sat up in bed and looked at him, coldly. "You are a booby," she said, "and I am going to have you put in a booby-hatch." The man, who never liked the words "booby" and "booby-hatch," and who liked them even less on a shining morning when there was a unicorn in the garden, thought for a moment. "We'll see about that," he said.

> a. Eudora Welty
> b. Shirley Jackson
> c. Thomas Wolfe
> d. F. Scott Fitzgerald
> e. Katherine Anne Porter
> f. James Thurber
> g. Ralph Ellison

Literature from the 1920s to the 1940s

The activities that follow are intended to extend your students' understanding and appreciation of the literature they have read in Unit One—Literature from 1920s to 1940s. They also provide a wide range of writing and thinking experiences. Be aware that all of these activities may not be suitable for all students.

Writing About Literature

1. If students could meet any character in one of these selections, which one would it be? Why? Have them write a two or three-paragraph explanation.

2. Ask students to write about the selection in this unit that was the most meaningful for them, explaining why.

3. Ask students to compare the writing styles of John Steinbeck and Ralph Ellison and write a few paragraphs analyzing their styles.

4. How would the story "Sucker" be different if Sucker himself had told it? Ask students to write a brief summary of the story as told from Sucker's point of view.

5. Invite students to choose one of the stories in this unit and update it for a modern-day movie or television program. Ask them to write a brief essay explaining how this would be done.

6. Invite students to write a "book review" of one of the stories in Unit One, critiquing it and recommending it (or not) to readers with justification.

7. Suggest that students consider what they have learned about American history from the 1920s to the 1940s. How do the stories in Unit One reflect what was going on in the country then? Ask students to write several paragraphs.

8. Hemingway's story takes place in Milan, and Fitzgerald's story is set in Paris. Compare the influence these two settings have on the stories "In Another Country" and "Babylon Revisited."

9. Invite students to find another story by James Thurber or Shirley Jackson, read it, and write a brief report that compares it to the author's selection in Unit One.

Writing Nonfiction

1. Tell students to look out an open window. Instruct them to take ten minutes to write a description of the sights, sounds, smells, and tastes in the air. Have them contrast their description with one of the settings in Unit One.

2. Have students choose one of the authors in this unit and write a brief biography of that person.

3. Have students write a description of how to play their favorite card or board game.

4. Ask students to write a descriptive paragraph that begins, "I have always been fascinated by . . . ."

5. Ask students to collect their favorite passages from the readings in this unit. Then ask them to choose two of these, rephrase them in their own words, and write an analysis of why these quotes are meaningful to them.

6. Encourage students to write a letter to their favorite author. They should tell the author why they admire his or her writing as well as something about themselves.

7. Ask students to read about what happened in one year between 1920 and 1940 in America and to write a short account of that year.

Creative Writing

1. Ask students to write a paragraph describing how they felt when they first read a piece of fiction with which they connected fully. Encourage them to use imaginative language and vivid images.

2. Invite students to choose one of the stories in Unit One and write an extension of the story that tells what happens after it ends.

3. Encourage imaginative students to write a story of their own time and place perhaps inspired by one of the stories or authors in Unit One.

4. Suggest that students write a newspaper story and headline about what happened during "The Lottery."

5. Have students consider the way each story in Unit One ends. Ask them to choose one story and write a totally different ending. Remind them that the ending has to remain true to the characters and situation.

6. Invite students to consider what they would do with a son like the one in "He." Have them write a short piece about how they would deal with the situation.

7. Let several volunteers work together to create a movie from one of the stories in Unit One. Ask them to create storyboards and a script.

8. Putting oneself in the place of a character is a good exercise in understanding characterization. Ask students to choose a character from one of the selections in Unit One and write a letter as that character to another character in the story. To expand the assignment, students might then write another letter as the character to a living political, literary, or cultural figure.

Writing Research Papers

1. Have students choose an author represented in Unit One and write a research paper about that author's life, work, major influences, and common themes.

2. Ask students to write a research paper about "The Lost Generation." Who were they? What did they believe in? What influenced them?

3. Suggest that interested students explore movies and television plays that have been made of the stories "the Lottery" and "The Secret Life of Walter Mitty." Ask them to write a paper that not only gives the information but also critiques the visual media versions and compares them to the written stories.

4. Ask students to research some of what has been written about Thomas Wolfe, his life and influences. Have them present their findings in a research paper.

5. Racial prejudice in America permeates the stories of Ralph Ellison. Invite students to discover more about how rampant it was in the 1920s and 1930s. Have them write a paper that describes what they find.

6. What with Fed Ex and the Internet, the days of the small, neighborhood post office may be numbered. Ask students to write a research paper comparing the United States Postal Service of today to the one in operation 50 years ago.

Presentations and Projects

1. Invite students who considered creating a movie from one of the Unit One stories work together to mock one up and present it to the rest of the class. They may choose to act it out, to present storyboards, to include sound effects, or even to make a video presentation.

2. Encourage groups of students to prepare a Readers Theatre piece based on one of the selections in this unit. Ask volunteers to perform their piece.

3. Ask students to draw a portrait of two characters from Unit One. Have them name each character and write a brief description of him or her. Display students' work in the classroom.

4. Let students with an auditory learning style make one of the stories into a radio play. Ask them to cast the characters with other students in the classroom and record the play, complete with sound effects, for all to hear.

5. Students with a kinesthetic learning style may get together and act out one of the stories as a play. Visually oriented students can participate with embellishments such as scraps of costumes, title boards, or even backgrounds done on bulletin- or chalkboards.

6. Suggest that students interested in music research some of the songs of the 1940s and present them to the class in whatever fashion they choose—some may sing, some may play instruments, others may simply play recordings from a library.

American Short Stories: Related Longer Works

Arranged by unit and difficulty level (RL = reading level)

UNIT I: LITERATURE FROM THE 1920s TO THE 1940s

The Member of the Wedding. Carson McCullers. The dark, confusing adolescent years of a young girl's debut into awareness. RL 6

The Winter of Our Discontent. John Steinbeck. An examination of the decline of moral standards in a society newly infected by the American dream of success. RL 6

East of Eden. John Steinbeck. A portrait of small-town life in the early 1900s. RL 7

Invisible Man. Ralph Ellison. A blazing story of a young Negro's experiences in the North and in the South. RL 7

Travels with Charley. John Steinbeck. Steinbeck sets out to rediscover his native land accompanied by his French poodle. RL 7

We Have Always Lived in the Castle. Shirley Jackson. Portrays the lives of two sisters after one is acquitted of the arsenic poisonings of four family members. RL 7

The Heart Is a Lonely Hunter. Carson McCullers. A cross-section view of humanity in a southern town. RL 7.7

In Cold Blood: A True Account of a Multiple Murder and Its Consequences. Truman Capote. Re-creation of the brutal slayings of the Clutter family of Holcolm, Kansas. RL 8

Of Mice and Men. John Steinbeck. A timeless novel of the love that men can feel for each other played out in the lives of two itinerant farm workers. RL 9

Juneteenth. Ralph Ellison. Posthumously published work that encompasses more than 40 years of Ellison's life, envisioned as his comment on race relations in the United States and told through the lives of two men whose lives were intertwined. Some strong language and adult situations. RL 10

The Great Gatsby. F. Scott Fitzgerald. Jay Gatsby challenges the powerful Eastern establishment while in pursuit of his romantic dream. RL 11

The Short Stories of F. Scott Fitzgerald: A New Collection. F. Scott Fitzgerald. This anthology contains 43 of Fitzgerald's best short fiction selections, with a preface and introductory headnotes by editor Matthew J. Bruccoli, the premier Fitzgerald scholar and biographer. RL 11

Tender Is the Night. F. Scott Fitzgerald. Fitzgerald's continued exploration of the American dream gone sour. RL 11

A Farewell to Arms. Ernest Hemingway. World War I story of an American ambulance driver on the Italian front and his love for a beautiful English nurse. RL 12

The Sun Also Rises. Ernest Hemingway. Story of an expatriate American newsman in the 1920s. RL 12

UNIT 2: LITERATURE FROM THE 1950s AND 1960s

The Autobiography of Miss Jane Pittman. Ernest J. Gaines. Depicts with touching simplicity the life of a black woman born into slavery. RL 4

Dandelion Wine. Ray Bradbury. The strange and wonderful worlds of Douglas Spalding, the supernatural, and the unknown. RL 5

Fahrenheit 451. Ray Bradbury. Story of a fireman of the future whose duty is not to put out fires, but to burn books. RL 7

A Lesson Before Dying. Ernest J. Gaines. Two black men—one a teacher, the other a death-row inmate—struggle to live and die with dignity. RL 7

A Gathering of Old Men. Ernest J. Gaines. When a white man in rural Louisiana is murdered, all the local black men claim responsibility for the murder. RL 8

A Good Man Is Hard to Find and Other Stories. Flannery O'Connor. Collection of ten short stories in which each main character faces an often violent conflict involving redemption and mercy. RL 8

The Illustrated Man. Ray Bradbury. Eighteen science fiction short stories that explore what it means to be human. RL 8

The Natural. Bernard Malamud. Portrait of a man adored and corrupted by the madcap world of major league baseball. RL 8

Slaughterhouse-Five. Kurt Vonnegut Jr. From the World War II firebombing of Dresden to the distant planet called Tralfamadore, the reader follows Billy Pilgrim in his attempt to understand the natures of time and existence. RL 9

The Sound and the Fury. William Faulkner. Saga told from four different points of view that traces the tragic decline of the once noble Compson family, descended from Civil War hero General Compson. RL 9

As I Lay Dying. William Faulkner. A poor white family takes the corpse of their mother to a distant burial ground. RL 10

Go Down Moses. William Faulkner. Faulkner's loosely related stories dealing with race relations in fictional Yoknapatawpha County in Mississippi. RL 10

Light in August. William Faulkner. Intertwining tales of Lena Grove, Lucas Burch, Byron Bunch, Joe Christmas, and Reverend Gail Hightower set in racially charged Yoknapatawpha County in Mississippi. RL 10

UNIT 3: LITERATURE FROM THE 1970s AND 1980s

A Day of Pleasure. Isaac Bashevis Singer. Autobiographical stories of the author's youth in Poland. Photographs. RL 6

The Color Purple. Alice Walker. Life wasn't easy for Celie, but she knew how to survive. Revealing truths about men and women, blacks and whites, God and love. Winner of the American Book Award and the Pulitzer Prize. RL 6

In Country. Bobbie Ann Mason. Recent high-school graduate Samantha (Sam) Hughes sets out to find out more about her father who was killed in the Vietnam War. Set in western Kentucky during the 1980s. RL 8

Joy Luck Club. Amy Tan. Sixteen interwoven stories depicting the conflict between immigrant mothers and their daughters raised in America as those daughters struggle to gain their own identities. RL 9

The Kitchen God's Wife. Amy Tan. Tan's second novel explores the dynamics of a Chinese American family through the long-suppressed secrets a mother and daughter ultimately reveal to each other. RL 9

The Temple of My Familiar. Alice Walker. A cross-cultural blend of fact and fiction about the remarkable strength of our own histories. RL 9

The Things They Carried. Tim O'Brien. An arc of fictional episodes that takes place in the childhoods of its characters, in the jungles of Vietnam, and back home in America two decades later. RL 9

The Bonesetter's Daughter. Amy Tan. Ruth Young struggles to understand her mother, who has been diagnosed with Alzheimer's disease, and in the process learns about her mother's past in a remote village in China and about herself. RL 10

UNIT 4: LITERATURE FROM THE 1990s

Big Mouth & Ugly Girl. Joyce Carol Oates. When 16-year-old Matt is falsely accused of threatening to blow up his high school and his friends turn against him, an unlikely classmate comes to his aid. RL 6

Old School. Tobias Wolff. A boy at an elite prep school wants more than anything to become a writer but must first learn to tell the truth about himself. A literary contest ignites strong competition, frays alliances, and exposes weaknesses, deceit, and betrayal. RL 6

The Bean Trees. Barbara Kingsolver. Attempting to break away from her harsh life in Appalachia, Taylor Greer finds herself in a small Oklahoma town with a new name, a new life, and, strangest of all, a new Cherokee baby girl that she names Turtle. RL 7.5

Good Scent from a Strange Mountain. Robert Olen Butler. A collection of short stories about Vietnamese immigrants living in Louisiana. RL 8

Pigs in Heaven. Barbara Kingsolver. Taylor wants to keep her adopted Cherokee daughter, but the Cherokee want her back. RL 8

Animal Dreams. Barbara Kingsolver. Blending flashbacks, dreams, and Native American legends, this book is a suspenseful love story and a moving exploration of life's largest commitments. RL 9

The Great Railway Bazaar. Paul Theroux. A travelogue that recounts Theroux's journey across Europe, the Middle East, the Indian Subcontinent, and Southeastern Asia by train. RL 9

The Lone Ranger and Tonto Fistfight in Heaven. Sherman Alexie. Twenty-two interconnected stories with recurring characters, including Victor Joseph and Thomas Builds-the-Fire—two Native American men living on the Spokane Indian Reservation. RL 9

The Poisonwood Bible: A Novel. Barbara Kingsolver. The wife and four daughters of a Baptist missionary tell the story of their family's three decades of epic struggles in postcolonial Africa detailing their tragic undoing and remarkable reconstruction. Includes a bibliography. RL 9

Prodigal Summer: A Novel. Barbara Kingsolver. Set in the mountains and on the struggling farms of southern Appalachia, this novel weaves together the stories of a reclusive wildlife biologist, a young farmer's wife, and a pair of elderly feuding neighbors. Some mature content. RL 9

The Road to Wellville. T. Coraghessan Boyle. Satire of 19th-century health practices. Set in Battle Creek, Michigan, during the early days of breakfast cereal, one plot line includes a caper to steal the recipe for cornflakes from John Harvey Kellogg, the inventor of cornflakes and the owner of a health spa. RL 9

This Boy's Life: A Memoir. Tobias Wolff. Memoir that traces the adolescence of Toby (a.k.a. Jake) Wolff, who moves with his divorced mother from Florida to Utah to Washington. When his mother remarries, Toby finds himself in a power struggle with his cruel stepfather. Toby tries reinventing himself to escape. RL 9

TABLE OF CONTENTS

PROLOGUE   DREAM VARIATION BY LANGSTON HUGHES   4

CREATING CONTEXT   9
from *Still Life in Harlem* by Eddy L. Harris • map of Harlem

CLUSTER ONE   WHAT WAS LIFE LIKE DURING
              THE HARLEM RENAISSANCE?
Thinking Skill   DESCRIBING

Seventh Avenue: The Great Black Way
JERVIS ANDERSON   essay   16

Laundry Workers' Choir
VIVIAN MORRIS   vignette   22

The Typewriter
DOROTHY WEST   short story   26

Rent Parties
FRANK BYRD   article   36

The Tropics in New York
CLAUDE MCKAY   poem   44

Harlem Wine
COUNTEE CULLEN   poem   45

RESPONDING TO CLUSTER ONE
Writing Activity   Creating Word Pictures   46

6

CLUSTER TWO WHAT DID HARLEM RENAISSANCE WRITERS SAY ABOUT BEING BLACK?

Thinking Skill ANALYZING

All God's Chillun Got Eyes
E. FRANKLIN FRAZIER   memoir   48

Race Pride
W. E. B. Du Bois   essay   52

I, Too
LANGSTON HUGHES   poem   55

Any Human to Another
COUNTEE CULLEN   poem   56

Black Men, You Shall Be Great Again
MARCUS GARVEY   essay   58

How It Feels to Be Colored Me
ZORA NEALE HURSTON   essay   62

The Pink Hat
CAROLINE BOND DAY   short story   68

A Black Man Talks of Reaping
ARNA BONTEMPS   poem   74

RESPONDING TO CLUSTER TWO
Writing Activity Encounter with the Past   76

CLUSTER THREE WHAT CONTRIBUTIONS WERE MADE TO AMERICAN ART AND CULTURE?

Thinking Skill GENERALIZING

The Negro Artist and the Racial Mountain
LANGSTON HUGHES   essay   78

Miss Cynthie
RUDOLPH FISHER   short story   86

***from* Ellington's "Mood in Indigo"**
JANET MABIE   article   100

7

Jazzonia
LANGSTON HUGHES   poem   105

RESPONDING TO CLUSTER THREE   106
Writing Activity Musical Poetry

CLUSTER FOUR THINKING ON YOUR OWN

Thinking Skill SYNTHESIZING

Spike's Gotta Do It
SPIKE LEE   journal   108

If Black English Isn't a Language, Then Tell Me, What Is?
JAMES BALDWIN   article   114

In Search of Zora Neale Hurston
ALICE WALKER   personal narrative   118

There's a Harlem Renaissance in My Head
MARUICE E. DUHON JR.   prose poem   141

RESPONDING TO CLUSTER FOUR   142
AUTHOR BIOGRAPHIES   143
ADDITIONAL READING   149

8

Three Teaching Options for *The Harlem Renaissance*

1- TO 2-WEEK UNIT

- Shorten the 4- to 6-week schedule by using one or more of the following strategies.
- Assign complete clusters to literary circles. Have each group share what they learn and/or teach the cluster to their classmates.
- Assign individual selections to groups. Have each group share what they learn and/or teach the selection to the entire class.
- Choose 8–13 significant selections for study by the entire class. The following list would provide a shortened exploration of the themes in *The Harlem Renaissance*.

Title	Page	Title	Page
Laundry Workers' Choir	22	How It Feels to Be Colored Me	62
Rent Parties	36	The Negro Artist and the Racial Mountain	78
The Tropics in New York	44	Miss Cynthie	86
All God's Chillun Got Eyes	48	Spike's Gotta Do It	108
Black Men, You Shall Be Great Again	58	There's a Harlem Renaissance in My Head	140

USING *THE HARLEM RENAISSANCE* WITH RELATED LITERATURE

Before Reading the Related Work

- Introduce the theme and the purpose for reading using the Anticipation Guide (page 60) of this teacher guide). From *The Harlem Renaissance* use the Preface (page 3), the Prologue (pages 4–5), and Creating Context (pages 9–14).
- Have students choose one or two selections and a poem to read from each cluster. Ask students to report on their selection and how it helped them answer the cluster question.

During Reading

- Ask students to relate the readings in *The Harlem Renaissance* to themes, actions, or statements in the longer work.
- At strategic points, have students discuss how characters in the longer work would react to selections in the anthology.

After Reading

- Have students read the last cluster and respond to the cluster questions, drawing upon selections in the anthology as well as the longer work.
- Ask students to compare and contrast one or more selections in the anthology and a theme in the longer work.
- Allow students to choose a research topic from the options given in **Research, Writing, and Discussion Topics** (page 55) or **Assessment and Project Ideas** (page 56).

Related Longer Works

The Portable Harlem Renaissance Reader edited by David L Lewis [RL 8 IL 9–12] Paperback 3995901.

The Crisis Reader: Stories, Poetry, and Essays from the N.A.A.C.P. Crisis Magazine edited by Sondra K. Wilson. [RL 9 IL 9–12] Paperback 3996101. Cover Craft 3996c102.

The Dream Keeper and Other Poems by Langston Hughes. [RL 6.1 IL 3–7] Paperback 8065401. Cover Craft 8065402.

See page 59 of this guide for more related titles.

Three Teaching Options for *The Harlem Renaissance*

4- TO 6-WEEK UNIT

Introducing the theme (1 to 2 days)

	Page Numbers In	
	Student Book	Teacher Guide

Read and discuss the following sections
- What Do You Think? (Anticipation Guide) 9, 60
- Preface 3 8
- Prologue 4–5 8
- Creating Context 9–14 9

Teaching the first three clusters (3 to 5 days per cluster)
- Introduce and model the cluster thinking skill using overhead/handout 11, 23, 37
- Pass out cluster vocabulary sheet 12, 24, 58
- Set schedule for reading selections in first three clusters
- For each selection, use appropriate discussion questions and extension activities
   - Cluster One 15–45 13–18
   - Cluster Two 47–75 25–32
   - Cluster Three 77–105 39–42
- As a class or in small groups discuss the **Responding to the Cluster** questions .... 46, 76, 106. .... 19, 33, 43
- Introduce Writing Activity with handout .... 46, 76, 106. .... 20, 34, 44
- Administer Vocabulary Test. 21, 35, 45

Teaching the last cluster (5 to 10 days)
The final section can be structured as a teacher-directed cluster or as independent learning. Choose from the two models described below.

Teacher-Directed
- Pass out cluster vocabulary sheet 49
- Set schedule for reading selections
- For each selection, use appropriate discussion questions and extension activities
- Administer Vocabulary Test. 50–53
- Assign research projects. 54
- Administer final essay test. 55–56 57

Independent Learning
Have students
- respond to one or more of the questions or activities on the Responding to Cluster Four page. 142
- plan and present a lesson over one or more of the selections in the last cluster 107–141
- conduct additional research on a related topic 55–56

TABLE OF CONTENTS

PROLOGUE   THE TIMES THEY ARE A-CHANGIN' BY BOB DYLAN   4

CREATING CONTEXT   9
The Swinging Sixties · A Dubious Crusade · Map of Southeast Asia ·
Timeline · Concept Vocabulary

CLUSTER ONE   What Were the Roots of the Conflict?   1 6
Thinking Skill   SUMMARIZING

FLASHBACK
Ballad of the Green Berets
SGT. BARRY SADLER   song lyrics   16

History
THUONG VUONG-RIDDICK   poem   18

The Gulf of Tonkin Resolution May Have
Been the Gulf Between Truth and Fiction
M. HIRSH GOLDBERG   article   20

Jack Smith
RON STEINMAN   oral history   23

On the Rainy River
TIM O'BRIEN   short story   33

RESPONDING TO CLUSTER ONE
Writing Activity A POETIC SUMMARY   4 8

CLUSTER TWO   What Was the War Experience?   4 9
Thinking Skill   ANALYZING

FLASHBACK
I-Feel-Like-I'm-Fixin'-To-Die Rag
JOE MCDONALD   song lyrics   50

6

Hippies
ALEX FORMAN — memoir — 52

Village
ESTELA PORTILLO TRAMBLEY — short story — 56

Farmer Nguyen
W. D. EHRHART — poem — 64

The Massacre at My Lai
HUGH THOMPSON — essay — 66

A Nun in Ninh Hoa
JAN BARRY — poem — 69

A Piece of My Heart
ANNE SIMON AUGER
AS TOLD TO KEITH WALKER — oral history — 70

RESPONDING TO CLUSTER TWO
Writing Activity SPINNING THE NEWS — 78

CLUSTER THREE **What Was Happening Back Home?** — 79
Thinking Skill GENERALIZING

FLASHBACK
San Francisco (Be Sure to Wear Some Flowers in Your Hair)
JOHN PHILLIPS — song lyrics — 80

Law and Order Chicago Style
DONALD KAUL — article — 82

Like a Rolling Stone
BEN FONG-TORRES — memoir — 85

Woodstock Nation
MARC ARONSON — essay — 88

Woodstock: The Oral History
IRWIN UNGER — interviews — 90

State of Emergency at "The People's Republic of Berkeley"
TOM HAYDEN — memoir — 94

7

Cambodia
PRESIDENT RICHARD M. NIXON — speech — 98

The Kent State Tragedy
ROGER BARR — article — 101

Born on the Fourth of July
from Born on the Fourth of July
RON KOVIC — autobiography — 103

RESPONDING TO CLUSTER THREE
Writing Activity DUELING LETTERS TO THE EDITOR — 108

CLUSTER FOUR **Thinking on Your Own** — 109
Thinking Skill SYNTHESIZING

FLASHBACK
Where Have All the Flowers Gone?
PETE SEEGER — song lyrics — 110

Epilogue
PHILIP CAPUTO — autobiography — 112

A President's Pain
PRESIDENT GERALD R. FORD — vignette — 117

The Summer of Vietnam
BARBARA RENAUD GONZALEZ — essay — 118

Stop the Sun
GARY PAULSEN — short story — 121

To Heal a Nation
JOEL L. SWERDLOW — article — 129

RESPONDING TO CLUSTER FOUR — 142
AUTHOR BIOGRAPHIES — 143
ADDITIONAL READING — 149

8

Three Teaching Options for *Times of Change*

	Page Numbers In	
	Student Book	Teacher Guide

4- to 6-Week Unit

Introducing the theme (1 to 2 days)

Read and discuss the following sections
- What Do You Think? (anticipation guide) 9, 65
- Preface 3 8
- Prologue 4–5 8
- Creating Context 9–14 9

Teaching the first three clusters (3 to 5 days per cluster)
- Introduce and model the cluster thinking skill using overhead/handout 11, 22, 35 13–17
- Pass out cluster vocabulary sheet. 12, 23, 36 24–30
- Set schedule for reading selections in first three clusters 37–44
- For each selection, use appropriate discussion questions and extension activities
  - Cluster One 16–47 13–17
  - Cluster Two 50–77 24–30
  - Cluster Three 80–107 37–44
- As a class or in small groups discuss the **Responding to the Cluster** questions .... 48, 78, 108 .... 18, 31, 45
- Introduce Writing Activity with handout .... 48, 78, 108 .... 19, 32, 46
- Administer Vocabulary Test 20, 33, 47

Teaching the last cluster (5 to 10 days)

The final section can be structured as a teacher-directed cluster or as independent learning. Choose from the two models described below.

Teacher-Directed
- Pass out cluster vocabulary sheet.
- Set schedule for reading selections
- For each selection, use appropriate discussion questions and extension activities 52–57
- Administer vocabulary test 51 58
- Assign research projects. 59–60
- Administer final essay test 61

Independent Learning

Have Students
- respond to one or more of the questions or activities on the Responding to Cluster Four page 142
- plan and present a lesson over one or more of the selections in the last cluster 110–141
- conduct additional research on a related topic 59–60

Three Teaching Options for *Times of Change*

1- to 2-Week Unit

Shorten the 4- to 6-week schedule by using one or more of the following strategies.
- Assign complete clusters to literary circles. Have each group share what they learn and/or teach the cluster to their classmates.
- Assign individual selections to groups. Have each group share what they learn and/or teach the selection to the entire class.
- Choose 8–10 significant selections for study by the entire class. The following list would provide a shortened exploration of the themes in *Times of Change*.

Title	Page	Title	Page
Jack Smith	23	A Piece of My Heart	71
On the Rainy River	35	Woodstock Nation	89
Hippies	53	The Summer of Vietnam	118
Farmer Nguyen	67	To Heal a Nation	129

USING *TIMES OF CHANGE* WITH RELATED LITERATURE

Before Reading the Related Work
- Introduce the theme and the purpose for reading using the Anticipation Guide (page 64 of this teacher guide). From *Times of Change* use the Preface (page 3), the Prologue (pages 4–5), and Creating Context (pages 9–16).
- Have students choose one or two selections and a poem to read from each cluster. Ask students to report on their selection and how it helped them answer the cluster question.

During Reading
- Ask students to relate the readings in *Times of Change* to themes, actions, or statements in the longer work.
- At strategic points, have students discuss how characters in the longer work would react to selections in the anthology.

After Reading
- Have students read the last cluster and respond to the cluster questions, drawing upon selections in the anthology as well as the longer work.
- Ask students to compare and contrast one or more selections in the anthology and a theme in the longer work.
- Allow students to choose a research topic from the options given in Research, Writing, and Discussion Topics (page 59) or Assessment and Project Ideas (page 60).

Related Longer Works

The Things They Carried by Tim O'Brien. [RL 9 IL 9 +] Paperback 4221501; Cover Craft 4221502.

In Country by Bobbie Ann Mason. [RL 8 IL 9 +] Paperback 4020201; Cover Craft 4020202.

Park's Quest by Katherine Paterson. [RL 5.5 IL 5–9] Paperback 4026301; Cover Craft 4026302.

See pages 3 of this guide for descriptions of these works and more related titles.

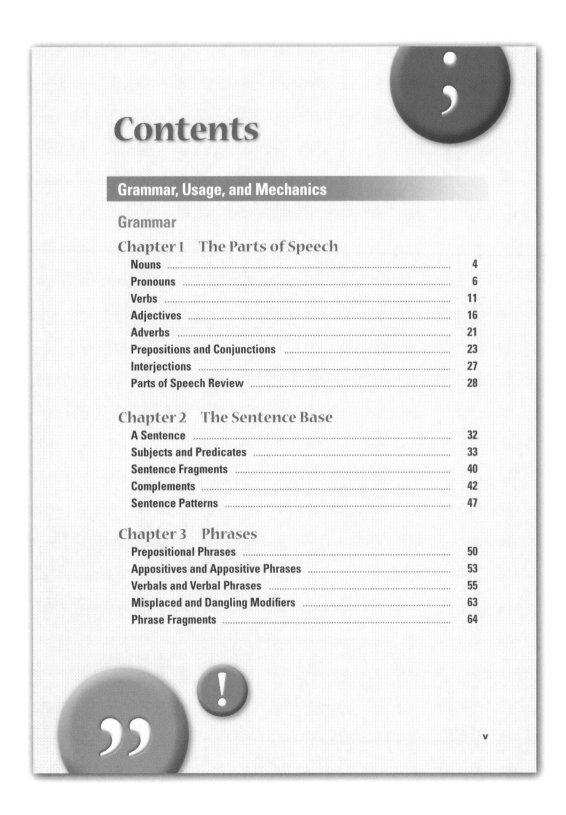

Contents

Grammar, Usage, and Mechanics

Grammar

Chapter 1   The Parts of Speech

Nouns 4
Pronouns 6
Verbs 11
Adjectives 16
Adverbs 21
Prepositions and Conjunctions 23
Interjections 27
Parts of Speech Review 28

Chapter 2   The Sentence Base

A Sentence 32
Subjects and Predicates 33
Sentence Fragments 40
Complements 42
Sentence Patterns 47

Chapter 3   Phrases

Prepositional Phrases 50
Appositives and Appositive Phrases 53
Verbals and Verbal Phrases 55
Misplaced and Dangling Modifiers 63
Phrase Fragments 64

v

Chapter 4   Clauses

Independent and Subordinate Clauses	68
The Uses of Subordinate Clauses	70
Sentence Structure	78
Clause Fragments and Run-on Sentences	81

Usage

Chapter 5   Using Verbs

Regular and Irregular Verbs	86
Six Problem Verbs	93
Verb Tense	96
Progressive and Emphatic Verb Forms	101
Voice	104
Mood	106

Chapter 6   Using Pronouns

The Cases of Personal Pronouns	110
Pronoun Problems	117
Pronouns and Their Antecedents	122

Chapter 7   Subject/Verb Agreement

Agreement of Subjects and Verbs	130
Common Agreement Problems	134
Other Agreement Problems	139

Chapter 8   Using Adjectives and Adverbs

Degrees of Comparison	146
Problems with Comparisons and Modifiers	150

A Writer's Glossary of Usage	156

Mechanics

Chapter 9   Capitalization

Capitalizing First Words and the Pronoun *I*	178
Capitalizing Proper Nouns and Proper Adjectives	180
Capitalizing Titles	185

Chapter 10   End Marks and Commas

End Marks in Sentences	190
Periods in Abbreviations and Outlines	192
Commas That Separate	194
Commas That Enclose	200

Chapter 11   Italics and Quotation Marks

Italics (Underlining)	206
Quotation Marks	209
Other Uses of Quotation Marks	214

Chapter 12   Other Punctuation

Apostrophes	218
Semicolons and Colons	223
Hyphens, Dashes, and Parentheses	227

Writing and the Six Traits

Chapter 13   Introduction to the Process of Writing

Using the Writing Process	234
Prewriting	236
Drafting	249
Revising	252
Editing	255
Publishing	259

vi

vii

Chapter 14   The Six Traits of Good Writing
Ideas 264
Organization 267
Voice 270
Word Choice 272
Sentence Fluency 274
Conventions 277

Chapter 15   Writing Strong Sentences
Prewriting 280
Drafting 282
Revising 285
Editing and Publishing 289

Chapter 16   Writing Powerful Paragraphs
Paragraph Structure 294
Writing Informative Paragraphs 298
Writing Other Types of Paragraphs 307

Chapter 17   Descriptive Writing
Writing to Describe 318
Prewriting 319
Drafting 325
Revising 327
Editing and Publishing 329

Chapter 18   Personal Writing
The Personal Narrative 332
Prewriting 333
Drafting 338
Revising 341
Editing and Publishing 343

viii

Chapter 19   Expository Writing
The Power of Expository Writing 346
Prewriting 347
Drafting 356
Revising 361
Editing and Publishing 363

Chapter 20   Persuasive Writing
Writing to Persuade 366
Prewriting 367
Drafting 375
Revising 377
Editing and Publishing 379

Chapter 21   Writing About Literature
The Literary Analysis 382
Prewriting 383
Drafting 399
Revising 402
Editing and Publishing 403

Chapter 22   Creative Writing
Writing Creatively 406
Writing a Story 407
Writing a Play 418
Writing a Poem 421
Revising 426
Editing and Publishing 429

Chapter 23   Writing the Research Paper
The Research Paper 432
Prewriting 443
Organizing 453
Using Sources 458
Drafting and Revising 472
Editing and Publishing 475

ix

xi

Communication

Chapter 24   Communication for College

The Application Process 478
Admission Letters and Applications ... 479
Interviewing 484

Chapter 25   Communication for the World of Work

The Business Letter 488
Seeking Employment: Letters and Résumés ... 491
Written Communication at Work 496

Chapter 26   Communication in the Digital Age

Communicating on the Internet 505
Information Sources on the Internet ... 509

Chapter 27   Speeches and Presentations

Preparing and Delivering a Speech or Presentation ... 513
Developing Your Critical Listening Skills ... 518
Participating in Group Discussions 520

Skill Building

Chapter 28   Vocabulary Power

The Varieties of English 523
Determining Word Meanings 527

Chapter 29   Critical Thinking

Thinking Skills 534
Logical Fallacies 543
Propaganda 549

Chapter 30   Spelling

Spelling Patterns 554
Plurals 556
Spelling Numbers 560

Chapter 31   Study Skills and Test-taking

Learning Study Skills 563
Taking Standardized Tests 568
Tests of Standard Written English 573
Taking Essay Tests 576

Literature

A Guide to Literature

Milestones in Literary History 582
Literary Masters 590
A Guide to Literary Genres 608
A Glossary of Literary Terms 616
The 100 Most Recommended Works 623
The 10 Most Recommended Authors ... 634
A Guide to Literary Analysis 636

Glossary of Grammar, Composition, and Thinking Skills ... 642

Index 648

x

CHAPTER 9 Capitalization

Pages 176–187

Skillbook and Assessment Resources

Skillbook Activities To reinforce the skills covered in this chapter, use the activities from the appropriate *Grammar, Usage, and Mechanics Skillbook*.

Level J (pages 254–276)

Level J (pages 215–233)

Level K (pages 187–204)

Level L (pages 233–249)

Chapter Test To assess your students' understanding of the skills and content covered in this chapter, use the test from the *Assessment Resources, Blue Level*.

Chapter 9 Test

Objectives
- To understand the rules for using capital letters
- To identify and correct errors in capitalization
- To use capital letters correctly in writing

Create Interest
Show students several magazine layouts or print advertisements that use nonstandard capitalization. Discuss the effects of using no capital letters, all capital letters, initial capital letters, or capitalization for emphasis. Explore whether longer blocks of type would be readable if they contained all capital letters or no capital letters.

Guided Instruction
Prompt students to write friendly letters, informative paragraphs, or a summary of cultural activities. Before students respond to the prompt, have them brainstorm proper nouns, proper adjectives, places, or titles that they are likely to use in their writing. Write several of these words on the board and review the rules for capitalizing them.

Connect to Everyday Life
Ask students to guess how long a typical employer spends reading a résumé. Remind them that a résumé is a document that summarizes a person's educational background and work experience. Résumés are usually one or two pages long. After students have stated their guesses, tell them that the average employer spends about 20 seconds scanning a résumé. Most will not bother to read a résumé with obvious errors in spelling, grammar, or capitalization. Ask students to discuss why they think this is true.

Collaborative Learning
Remind students that critics like to come up with lists like the 10 Best Movies of All Time or the People's Choice awards. Brainstorm lists of titles that students might like to create, whether it's the best episodes of a particular show, their own class list of favorite books, or the top forty hits. Work with the group to develop a survey. Assign each student to survey five people and tally and proofread the results. Compile the results and post the final list.

Capitalizing First Words and the Pronoun I (pages 178–179)

The Differentiated Classroom

English Language Learners While many languages use capitalization, some do not. Asian students in particular may need extra reinforcement of English capitalization conventions. Students may also need to pay particular attention to the way pronouns are capitalized in English. For example, the German and Dutch languages capitalize some forms of *you*. In addition, English is the only language that capitalizes the pronoun *I* when it does not appear at the beginning of a sentence. If students need extra practice, have them write the sentences below with correct capitalization. Follow up by having students identify words that change their meaning, depending on whether they are capitalized or not. Examples include *sue, bill, turkey,* and *pat.*

"sue, ask bill to bring the potato chips." ("Sue, ask Bill to bring the potato chips.")

"i will," said sue, "and i'll bring vegetables and dip." ("I will," said Sue, "and I'll bring vegetables and dip.")

"mel will bring turkey sandwiches." ("Mel will bring turkey sandwiches.")

"i can hardly wait to welcome pat back from her trip to turkey." ("I can hardly wait to welcome Pat back from her trip to Turkey.")

Auditory Learners Tell students that some professional proofreaders work with partners. One person follows the text as the other reads it aloud, including the names of all capital letters and punctuation marks. The person following the text marks any corrections that are needed. Ask students to follow along as you read the possible corrections to the following sentence.

the test is tomorrow

a. the test is tomorrow [period].

b. [capital T] The test is tomorrow [period].

Ask students if they noted any errors in either item.

Advanced Learners Ask students to work with partners or in small groups to write original words to an existing melody. Before they write or type the final draft, ask students to discuss whether they want to use conventional or nonconventional capitalization in their song. Have them include a brief note about their decision and the reasons for it at the end of their song.

Collaborative Learning
Tell students that a dictionary can answer many questions about capitalization. Assign each student a letter of the alphabet. Have them skim the dictionary entries for that letter and make up five questions that their classmates can answer by referring to the dictionary. Tell them to make their questions more challenging by choosing some entries that are capitalized and some that are not. Then have students exchange papers and answer a classmate's questions. Discuss what students learned from writing and answering the questions.

The Differentiated Classroom

Advanced Learners Help students understand the difference between categories and particular members of the category by creating a ladder of abstraction. Such ladders move from an abstract idea through increasingly specific subcategories to a particular member of the most specific subcategory. Show students the example below.

Cities

International cities

European cities

European cities where French is spoken

Paris

Work with students to create another ladder of abstraction, beginning with the idea of space and working down to their particular location. Discuss which items on each ladder should be capitalized.

Capitalizing Proper Nouns and Proper Adjectives (pages 180–184)

Proper Nouns (pages 180–184)

The Differentiated Classroom

Visual Learners Tell students that writers who create perfect worlds, or utopias, often draw a map of their ideal world. Ask them to think about their perfect world. Would it be an island? a continent? a river basin? Then have students make a sketch of their world, including at least five different geographic features, such as towns, sections of a country, and bodies of water. Tell students that the geographical names they choose should reflect the nature of their utopia, such as Cooperation City or Mount Individual Effort. Remind them that because the maps are intended for people in our world, geographic names should follow the conventions of capitalization.

Collaborative Learning

Have students work through the following sentences with a partner. The first student should read the first sentence and identify the capital letters needed. If the answer is correct, the second student should accept it. If the answer is incorrect, the second student should offer hints to help find the correct answer or provide the answer and explain why it is correct. Students should then switch roles and continue switching roles after every item.

recently in a letter from my aunt, I learned that the o'tooles have been traveling across the country.

they crossed the mississippi river last week.

the o'tooles have learned about the many countries that have influenced texas: spain, france, and mexico.

last week they are planning to visit sacramento, california.

last night they watched venus rise as they drove east on rte. 44.

we got a postcard from the painted desert.

the o'tooles plan to travel to china, japan, and parts of the middle east next year.

on their last trip, they saw the home of ulysses s. grant and discovered that his horse was named egypt.

Integrating Technology

Internet Tell students that local chambers of commerce often have brochures of landmarks and scenic attractions that visitors might like to see. Ask students to make a list of landmarks or attractions that might appear on a Web site hosted by a chamber of commerce in their area. Follow up by listing all the suggested attractions on the board and having students check their spelling and capitalization.

Word Processing Word processing software allows different capitalization styles to be applied to text. Options might include initial capital letters, small caps, and title case. Have students apply five different capitalization options to a paragraph or short essay. Ask them to print out the results and ask at least five people to rate them from 1 (most readable) to 5 (least readable).

Collaborative Learning

Have students work in groups to develop a visitor's guide to their area. Ask them to develop a written overview that includes an outline of what their guide will include and a discussion of its format — brochure, Web page, or newspaper advertisement. Have students submit their overviews for approval. As you review their plans, look for possible audiences for their work. For example, a Web page might be linked to a site hosted by the school or an organization that serves tourists.

Collaborative Learning

Use a Graphic Organizer Ask students to make a timeline that includes at least five important historical events that have happened during their lifetime. Have individuals contribute their ideas to a group timeline, which should include any events the group finds significant. Follow up by discussing events students chose and identifying which events should be capitalized. If students disagree about whether an event should be capitalized, suggest that they refer to the guidelines for capitalizing specific time periods and events and to reference sources such as encyclopedias and history textbooks.

The Differentiated Classroom

Struggling Learners Help students apply what they are learning by making a list of events or proper nouns that they are studying in one of their content-area classes. Display the list in the classroom. Each day, go over a few items from the list and review the capitalization rules that apply to those items.

Auditory Learners Use the ten items below as a dictation exercise. Ask students to write each item as you read it, capitalizing correctly. You might want to identify each term with a label. For example, after saying "an Italian," you might say, "Italian is a nationality." Then read each item a second time to allow students to check their spelling and capitalization.

1. an Italian
2. Buddhism
3. Easter
4. the Grammy Awards
5. the Lincoln Memorial
6. the ship *Titanic* (award extra credit for underlining Titanic)
7. a Spaniard
8. Yom Kippur
9. the Brooklyn Bridge
10. a Greek goddess

Integrating Technology

Netiquette Ask students if they are familiar with the Netiquette for using capital letters. (*Netiquette* means the rules of courtesy when communicating on the Internet.) Netiquette considers using all capital letters in an e-mail message the equivalent of shouting, which is rude.

Proofreading for Capital Letters

Write the sentence below on the board. Introduce students to the page of proofreader's marks on page 258, particularly the marks for capital letter and lowercase. Have them use the marks to correct the sentence.

the alamo, the old spanish mission founded in 1718 at san antonio, texas, was the site of one of the most famous Sieges in all of united states History.

Proper Adjectives (page 184)

The Differentiated Classroom

Linguistic Learners Ask students to identify their ethnic backgrounds. Write the proper adjectives for each ethnic background on the board. Then find out how many people in the class share each ethnic background. Write the number beside each proper adjective. Discuss why words such as Irish, Hispanic, or African American are capitalized. You may need to remind students that proper adjectives are formed from proper nouns.

Visual Learners Write these incorrect examples on the board. Have students use proofreaders' marks to correct the errors.

french pastries

hungarian waltz

Swedish Meatballs

German Shepherd

African american

Irish Dancing

Alaskan Folklore

russian accent

Capitalizing Titles (pages 185–187)

The Differentiated Classroom

English Language Learners Help students become familiar with the forms of address. Explain that *Mr.*, *Mrs.*, *Miss*, and *Ms.* are polite forms of address that are used with a person's last name. Discuss situations in which students should use the polite forms of address.

Linguistic Learners Ask students to write down the names and titles of five important people they have learned about in their content-area classes. Write the names and titles on the board, and have students check the spelling and capitalization.

Workplace Writing

Show students some examples of business cards. Point out that the name of the business and the title of the person named on the card are usually capitalized. (Exceptions might include graphic artists or high-tech companies; to show their creativity, they often deliberately break convention.) Ask students to consider what they might be doing two years after they graduate and to create a business card that would be appropriate for that job.

Collaborative Learning

Using a Graphic Organizer Ask students to create a poster or graphic organizer that illustrates one of the rules of capitalization. Display the results to reinforce the importance of using correct capitalization.

Collaborative Learning

Have students work with partners or in small groups to create original sentences that show how to capitalize titles used alone, titles showing family relationships, and titles of written works and other works of art.

Stumbling Blocks

Problem: Using too many capital letters in titles

Solution: Remind students that capitalization is used to create emphasis by giving certain words more importance than others. If everything is capitalized, the emphasis is lost.

Point out to students that words other than proper nouns, proper adjectives, and titles are generally not capitalized. Point out that articles, coordinating conjunctions, and prepositions of fewer than five letters are generally not capitalized unless they begin or end a title.

66 Grammar, Usage, and Mechanics

MATRIX
Program Titles

Many Voices Literature Anthology Titles 61

Literature & Thought Titles 62

Parallel Text Titles 65

Retold Titles 65

Many Voices Literature Anthology Titles

There are seven focused anthologies in the Matrix program. The first three titles below are generally selected for middle school classrooms.

THEMES: AN INTRODUCTION TO LITERATURE
A well-chosen mix of classic, contemporary, and young adult literature that presents the elements of each genre along with special emphasis on vocabulary and reading skills.

SNAPSHOTS: LITERATURE FOR YOUNG ADULTS
The best of young adult literature from the best of young adult authors. Each of the thematic units concentrates on one of six active reading strategies: questioning, predicting, clarifying, connecting, summarizing, evaluating.

A MULTICULTURAL READER: COLLECTION ONE
Every student will find himself or herself within the pages of this reader-friendly anthology. Issues of family, traditions, growing up in a multicultural society, and living with a foot in two different cultures are some of the themes presented.

A MULTICULTURAL READER: COLLECTION TWO
Although patterned on Collection One, selections in this second volume of contemporary multicultural literature are more challenging and sophisticated. Unit Reviews present thought-provoking discussion questions, debate topics, and composition assignments, and encourage students to "tell their own story" in writing.

READING THE WORLD:
CONTEMPORARY LITERATURE FROM AROUND THE GLOBE
An intriguing and enlightening collection of literature chosen to provide a broader world perspective for students. Selections, arranged according to geographical region, focus on both differences and similarities between Americans and citizens of other countries. The anthology invites students not only to "read the world," but also to research it. An extensive research handbook to assist in writing research papers is included.

THE AMERICAN TRADITION: SHORT STORIES FROM 1820 TO 1920
A classic collection of short fiction representing America's literary heritage with special emphasis on master writers such as Hawthorne, Poe, Twain, Crane, and Cather. Before- and after-reading instruction focuses on literary elements and analysis.

AMERICAN SHORT STORIES: 1920 TO THE PRESENT
A highly interesting and highly challenging "best of the best" collection showcases contemporary writers decade by decade. This unique text approaches selections based on the analysis of each author's particular writing style. In addition, the text encourages students to develop their own writing style.

Literature & Thought Titles

These mini-anthologies are appropriate for a 1- to 2-week unit of study. This series is specially focused on learning through inquiry and developing critical thinking skills.

LITERARY GENRES

Echoes from Mt. Olympus (mythology)
Essential Question: Why do myths endure?
Thinking Skills: Generalizing, Comparing/Contrasting, Evaluating, Synthesizing

Flights of Fantasy
Essential Question: Why read fantasy?
Thinking Skills: Defining, Analyzing, Evaluating, Synthesizing

The Main Event (sports)
Essential Question: What is the value of sport?
Thinking Skills: Defining, Analyzing, Inferring, Synthesizing

Mysterious Circumstances (mystery)
Essential Question: Why are we fascinated by mystery?
Thinking Skills: Defining, Investigating, Logical Thinking, Synthesizing

The Sci-Fi Factor (science fiction)
Essential Question: What's the fascination with science fiction?
Thinking Skills: Analyzing, Hypothesizing, Drawing Conclusions, Synthesizing

What on Earth? An Ecology Reader
Essential Question: How do we protect our planet?
Thinking Skills: Evaluating, Analyzing, Problem Solving, Synthesizing

What's So Funny? (humor)
Essential Question: What's so funny?
Thinking Skills: Evaluating, Analyzing, Classifying, Synthesizing

LITERARY THEMES

And Justice for All (justice/fairness)
Essential Question: What is justice?
Thinking Skills: Evaluating, Analyzing, Comparing/Contrasting, Synthesizing

The Best of Friends (friendship)
Essential Question: What is the value of friendship?
Thinking Skills: Defining, Analyzing, Evaluating, Synthesizing

Decisions, Decisions (decision-making)
Essential Question: How do I make a decision?
Thinking Skills: Analyzing, Evaluating, Predicting, Synthesizing

Family Matters
Essential Question: Does family matter?
Thinking Skills: Defining, Comparing/Contrasting, Evaluating, Synthesizing

On the Edge of Survival
Essential Question: What can be learned from survival literature?
Thinking Skills: Hypothesizing, Generalizing, Evaluating, Synthesizing

To Be a Hero
Essential Question: Who can be a hero?
Thinking Skills: Classifying, Analyzing, Evaluating, Synthesizing

Who Am I? (identity)
Essential Question: Who's the real you?
Thinking Skills: Defining, Analyzing, Evaluating, Synthesizing

HISTORICAL EVENTS AND ERAS

Dark Days: America's Great Depression
Essential Question: What was the Great Depression?
Thinking Skills: Evaluating, Summarizing, Analyzing, Synthesizing

Free At Last: The Struggle for Civil Rights
Essential Question: How do we achieve the ideal of equal rights for all?
Thinking Skills: Analyzing, Evaluating Cause and Effect, Comparing/
Contrasting, Synthesizing

From There to Here: The Immigrant Experience (immigration)
Essential Question: Should we keep America's immigration door open?
Thinking Skills: Investigating, Analyzing, Comparing/Contrasting, Evaluating,
Synthesizing

The Harlem Renaissance
Essential Question: What was the Harlem Renaissance?
Thinking Skills: Describing, Analyzing, Generalizing, Synthesizing

A House Divided: America's Civil War
Essential Question: Why is the Civil War considered a defining moment in American history?
Thinking Skills: Generalizing, Comparing/Contrasting, Evaluating, Synthesizing

Times of Change: Vietnam and the 60s
Essential Question: What effect did the decade of the 60s have on the United States?
Thinking Skills: Summarizing, Analyzing, Generalizing, Synthesizing

Voices of the Holocaust
Essential Question: Could a Holocaust happen here?
Thinking Skills: Analyzing, Comparing/Contrasting, Generalizing, Synthesizing

Wide Open Spaces: American Frontiers (Westward expansion)
Essential Question: What is the lure of the frontier?
Thinking Skills: Analyzing, Comparing/Contrasting, Summarizing, Synthesizing

Parallel Text Titles

Perfection Learning *Parallel Texts* present unabridged Shakespeare and other classic literature in a side-by-side format: original language on the left-hand page and a modern translation on the right. Titles include:

Romeo and Juliet
Julius Caesar
Macbeth
Hamlet
Othello
The Taming of the Shrew
King Lear
The Merchant of Venice
A Midsummer Night's Dream
Early American Literature
British Literature, 449–1798

Retold Titles

Retold texts are, as the name implies, retellings that make important literature accessible to challenged or reluctant readers. The wide range of genres includes mythology and short story collections, as well as frequently taught novels. Following is a partial list of titles:

CLASSIC NOVELS
Frankenstein
Huckleberry Finn
The Red Badge of Courage
The Scarlet Letter
A Tale of Two Cities
Treasure Island

MYTHOLOGY AND FOLKLORE
African American Myths
African Myths
Asian Myths
Classic Myths, Vols. 1, 2, and 3
Mexican American Myths
Native American Myths
Northern European Myths
World Myths

ANTHOLOGIES
American Classics, Vols. 1, 2, and 3
American Hauntings
British Classics
Edgar Allan Poe
Jack London
Mark Twain
Sherlock Holmes
World Classics

Notes